As After Sunset Fadeth in the West

As After Sunset Fadeth in the West

A MEMOIR IN POETRY AND PROSE

BY RICHARD HOLT

As After Sunset Fadeth in the West: A Memoir in Poetry and Prose
Copyright © 2018 by Richard Holt

All rights reserved. No part of this book may be used or reproduced in any form, electronic or mechanical, including photocopying, recording, or scanning into any information storage and retrieval system, without written permission from the author except in the case of brief quotation embodied in critical articles and reviews.

Book design by Madison Feldhaus

Printed in the United States of America

The Troy Book Makers • Troy, New York • thetroybookmakers.com

To order additional copies of this title,
contact your favorite local bookstore
or visit www.shoptbmbooks.com

ISBN: 978-1-61468-443-5

Dedicated to Lisa

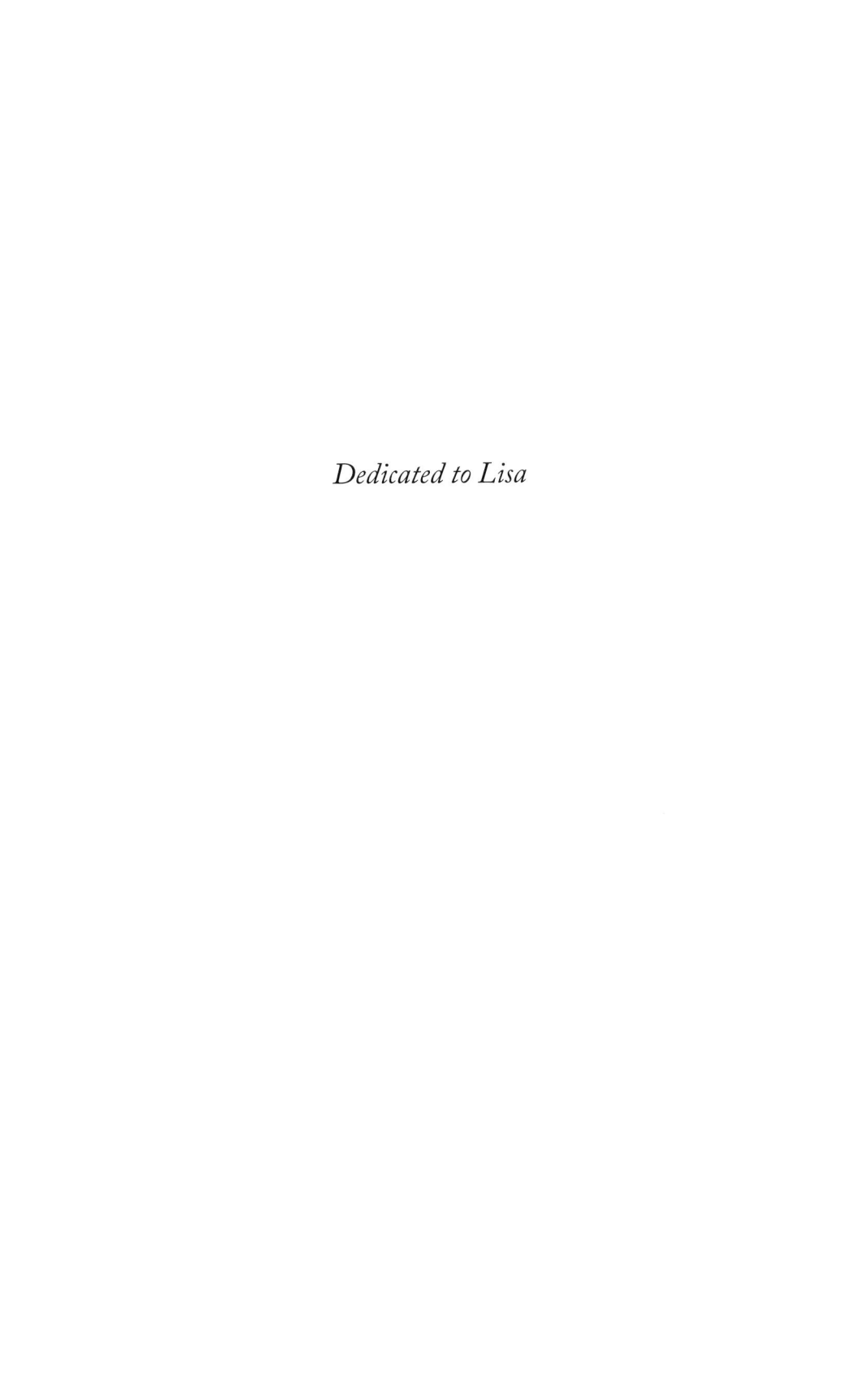

Contents

Introduction

Prose & Poetry
Shaking Branches 4
A Memory Closet 6
Growing up in a Rooming House 7
Dorothy's Words 18
Victory Lake 20
Sunset and Evening Star 21
Vincent 23
The Sun's in My Heart 24
Sacred Stones: East Park, NY 26
A Winking Eye 27
P.O. 28
The Old Cabin 31
Bingo 32
Sons 34
Lleyton 2015 35
To Sara 1975 36
To Lucie 2015 37
Cora at 3 38
The Greyhound Station 1969 39
Crouse College, S.U. 1977 40
Omniscience 41
All in Light 42
Fleeting 43
The Last Syllable 44
Life in Limbo 45
October Drive 1980 46
Eternal Sunrise 47
The Escape of Summer 48
Ode to PHS 50
Infatuation 52
A Last Round 1990 53
Playing Lahinch 1997 54
A Leaner 63

Cafeteria Cutie 1989 65
Teaching Dreams 66
A Tribute to Bob Williams 67
She Soars: to Linda Witkowski 69
A New Old Flame 70
Rediscovery 72

With
Chance? 74
Dream Folly 78
Irish Love Song 79
Cape Magic 80
Sea Spray 81
Brewster Flats 82
From Plymouth to P-Town 84

Without
A Run 88
Flannel Dreams 89
A Gray Day in December 90
Frozen Redeemer 91
Westport: The First Thanksgiving 92
Chant 93
Winter Limbo (January 2015) 94
Layers 95
Naples FL: A Winter Reverie 96
Emotional Rescue 97
A Smile Once More 98
Thoughts From the Pew 99
Seeking 101
Cuba Libre 102
Sunsets for Christmas 104
The Close 106
Chapter by Chapter 107
Acknowledgements 109
Sonnet 73 by William Shakespeare .. 111

Introduction

Every English teacher is a closet writer. For years of school, graduate school, and teaching we teach and think about composition. We defer our own writing desire for work, relationships, marriage and children. And then with family, we assume other duties, teach other classes and coach for that little extra. Writing is a luxury most of us can't afford.

As an undergraduate, I took my first creative writing class with Dr. O.Howard Winn. I loved it but I was a poor imitator of my idols from Brit Lit: "she walks in beauty, like the night."

Thank you Lord Byron. The Romantics and Victorian were my models: "Flower in the crannied wall, I pluck you out of the cranny." My final paper for the course was a terrible tale of a white game hunter (Hemingway) obsessed with hunting a one eyed jaguar. Thank you Melville! I received a C+ which I deserved, Dr.Winn.

My teaching at Niskayuna High School gave me many opportunities to garner ideas for writing. My classes were full of teen-agers whose complexity caused me to reflect not only on the promise of youth but on my own attempt to grow up. I taught with an amazing staff. John Hogan, Lillian Turner and Linda Witkowski to name only a few. John hired me in 1970 and that started me on a great run, at a great school. I was able to teach Creative Writing and a Shakespeare elective that were high points of my career. One colleague, Karen Ludwig, with whom I shared so much, pushed me into applying for a Summer fellowship at Tufts University titled Life History Writing. There I met interesting teachers from across the country who had so many stories to tell and who impressed me with the importance of memoir writing.

In the lettuce days of marriage, the only writing I did was journaling of the children, reflecting on my life thus far, and travel. As the kids got older and went away to school, my travel journals became a record of our experience and life together. Still, Lisa encouraged me to write. Since she failed to marry a Senator, although I was elected to our Town Council, I think she hoped for a novelist. As a librarian and life-long reader she loved books, even those I had yet to write.

I journaled our wonderful trips to England, Ireland, France, Italy and Greece. I reflected on teaching which still haunts my dreams in retirement. I related my perspective on the amazing journeys that we took with Marion Burns and the "Walkers." The journal became one of my escapes and a catharsis as Lisa was diagnosed with cancer. And it was a venue for my grieving process through the first year.

So here it is. A memoir. A collection of poetry, and essay, all a part of my personal life history. Verse that spans my years. The story of the house where I grew up, my British grandfather. reflections of my mother and the role of chance in shaping my story.

I hope that readers will see me in one genre or the other and know me for who I was and who I am.

Rich

Prose & Poetry

Shaking Branches

On warm summer nights, when I was twelve, I slipped from my bed

    And slowly, silently slid up the screen of my bedroom window,

And like an escaping cat burglar stepped out onto the flat metal roof

    To become a part of the dark night and ride the summer breezes.

Slowly I'd walk barefoot to the edge.

    There before me the large chestnut tree took shape.

The five leafed palms limbs reached out to me as if to greet an old friend.

    They rustled in the blackness.

Even now can I close my eyes and see myself leaping out to grab a limb

      And nuts showering the yard below.

From limb to limb I soar higher and higher,
shaking branches

      until the green spikey kernals cover the ground.

Up and back to the roof I fly, my Peter Pan trip done

      And return to bed.

A dream of peeled red nuts litters my blankets.

      Some to carve out with my pocket knife,

Others to throw at unsuspecting kids

      And more to pile into pyramids,

And one that rolls under my pillow for good luck.

A Memory Closet

When I was small, my cavernous closet was a treasure chest in which to hide,

> both my toys and feelings deep inside.

A bare bulb cut into the dark when I stretched high to pull the chain.

> Like the sun coming out from the clouds, it shone on the objects below.

Other times I just went by the light of the open door and shadows entered with me as my only companions.

They cast swaying patterns on all that was within:

> My baseball bat and mitt,
>
> The rubber banded cards, bound up as teams,
>
> The old box that held my Lionel train and miles, I thought, of track.
>
> My Red Ryder bb rifle and numerous cap guns,
>
> World War II plaster cast soldiers,
>
> Lead WW I fighters that my Dad had played with,
>
> A tank that had lost its tread,
>
> A shoot down the Mescherschmitt game that kept me flying for hours.

And largest of all, Pep the wooden rocking horse once loved, now living in a dark stable.

Growing up in a Rooming House

For several years, I have gone back to Mansion Street in memory, hoping to recover some of the increasingly distant past. Pages are written, pages are lost. Thoughts are uncovered, yet many lie hidden beneath a layer of dust so thick, it might as well be in the cemetery of my mind. "Dig, dig, dig," dreamed Dr. Mannette in Dickens's classic, and so must I.

We came to 300 Mansion Street sometime after the death of my father and the sale of my Grandmother's house on Hamilton Street. Perhaps 1949. My mom's mother was a colorful Gram. Francis Matilda Wilson, or Tilly as we called her was a shaping force on me. She was a survivor of divorce and worked hard at life; she rented rooms in 300 as a source of income but she also worked as a seamstress in a coat factory and checked coats part-time at a local bowling alley. On the weekends, she and her younger sister Rita would dress up to hit local bars. Both had dyed red hair and were considered wild. She once was thrown out of a local watering hole, The Brass Rail, for punching a guy off his stool after he put his hand on her knee. Now that mom was a widow, she was available to run 300. And she welcomed the offer of a second home for my older brother and me.

In addition to housework Mom had to walk me to kindergarten at the dark brown, looming building which was Morse School where I was destined to return for 8th grade. My new school, Warring for first grade, was across the street from 300, Tillie's new house and our new home. I flew high on the swings in the school playground attempting to rotate a 360 degree arc until I was too old to be there. I survived hide and go seek at dusk with the older kids. I took an old broomstick to play stickball at the back of the building and shot my first baskets into the chain-metal nets of the small court. The most intimidating game for a shy kid was a form of tag in which the guy who became "it" was de-pantsed by the rest of the guys. I may have only played a couple times in my pre-teen years before one of the tougher guys started to throw fists at his captors. I fled to the sanctuary of my own porch.

Going home for lunch was easy. Although crossing in the middle of the block was against the rules, I soon outgrew the crossing guard at the corner and could run down the sloping walk of Warring to cross in the middle and run up the stairs and into my front door before I was noticed. Both buildings became my homes. My mother worked three jobs but made a point to come back to have lunch with me. However, I was often on my own. Her first job was for the small grocery on the corner of Smith and Mansion, the Skinners. In those days, the neighborhood supported two small grocery stores within a hundred feet of each other. Leaving there after morning hours at the counter, she went to work at the cleaners on lower Mansion Street, where she formed a long relationship with Sadie Taub, the large Jewish proprietor. The third and perhaps most important job was that Dorothy, my Mom, ran the rooming house for Tillie, by washing, cleaning and cooking for the family as well as those special people who rented a room from my grandmother for the princely sum of eight dollars a week. These "boarders" became part of my memories of 300 and left an indelible mark on my growing up.

A dashing French-Italian from the City, Guy Mule, was perhaps the most notable of the boarders, because he became part-of-the-family. With no male parent in our house, Guy, who was at least forty and never having had children of his own, took a welcome interest in me and my brothers. He was an imperfect model for me, imperfect only, because he kept late hours, drank and smoked and last, ran away with another man's wife. However, the fact was that he could do no harm in the eyes of both my mother and grandmother and we loved him. We were among the many that had been charmed by him whether he was bringing Dottie a special cut of meat from The Bull Market where he was a meat cutter or when he popped into our living room impeccably dressed before he went out on a date. He would simply knock and then enter. No other boarder ever had such license. He often sat and talked and laughed with us. In those days of smoking, my mother gladly provided the ash tray for his cigarette. On the weekends, he might stop to share a Ballantine beer with my older brothers or "Mom Holt." He was a good listener and even better talker, regaling us with tales of customers who had come into the store or anecdotes of New York City and work on the docks as a longshoreman. He had a scar on one cheek which my brother told me was the work of a baling hook and in my imagination, the mark of bravery or at least an attack by the bad guys who worked along the East River such as I had seen in a Marlon Brando movie.

I confess—I was a snoopy kid. There were frequent times when I was alone in the large house, my mother working and my brothers pursuing their version of adolescence, and like a spy, I thought, climbed quietly to Guy's third floor bedroom and tried to imagine his life by the things on his dresser, his clothes and by what he read. I would pick up things and return them to the same spot so he would have no idea that someone had been snooping. A cigarette pack, cufflinks, after shave lotion that according to my older brother made Guy smell like a French whore as if that made sense to me, and an occasional note or two, reminders to do things or dates about which I could only imagine. Here I picked up what I later learned to be a foil wrapped condom whose use I had no idea about until instructed by another roomer yet to take up residence.

Guy would come home still wearing the white robe of his trade, often spotted with the blood of that day's beef shipment. Extra robes hung on the coat rack in his room until my mother would pick them up to wash with the linens for the week. Later that day, they would be returned to his bed folded neatly. She didn't do personal work for the rest of the roomers, but Guy was special. He was probably too old to be her son and so he flirted with her and at the same time that she pushed him away, she was exhilarated by his attention. She was still a young widow and while not seeking the attention of men, fell victim to a couple during my childhood. But, that's another story.

Guy's dates often involved a drive over the Mid-Hudson bridge to Highland and Newburgh which must have been perilous journeys in the early morning light after a night of partying. Sometimes he would be at the door, which was only locked after dark, fumbling with the keys. While Tillie warned him, it was more like being scolded by his mother. It was not until he had a close call, hitting a tree on a treacherous curve in Marlboro that his life turned in another direction.

After the crash, Tillie and I raced to St. Luke's Hospital, slowing down a moment to view the tree which was quite scarred by its encounter with Guy's old Chevie. At the hospital, he managed a smile through his stitched face that notched his Sicilian complexion. Still, he flirted with the nurses, with my Grandmother and with the nuns. When Tillie called him "a damn fool," he responded with, "I love you too." And when he was released, after a few days, it was Tillie who drove down to Newburgh. Guy limped out to her 1952 Ford and we brought him back to 300.

For several weeks he had to be driven or was picked up by taxis to go to work. Once when I answered the doorbell, he was picked up by a pretty girl who smelled like lilacs. His life was quiet for at least a month until he told my mother of meeting a woman at work, one of his customers. Not long after, he appeared in the hallway to announce that he was taking a trip and would call. His rent had been paid for two weeks. I listened into all the talk that this generated; we all waited to hear what the next part of the story would be.

It wasn't two weeks before we got a call from Reno asking my mother to see that the rest of his belongings were sent west. He was staying. Guy had run off with a married woman, and she had gotten a Reno divorce from her husband who was a deputy sheriff in Pleasant Valley. He asked Dottie to box his remaining possessions and mail them off. My Grandmother only smiled and shook her head. "That devil, Guy. Now maybe his skirt chasing days will be over." And they were.

I didn't see him until several years later, when I was twenty-four; I went across country with Ed and slept on the floor of Guy's home in Los Vegas. The night was at least 90 degrees and Guy took us out, much to the interest of his young children to see the town. Sometime in the next five years he and his family moved back to Pine Plains in Dutchess County, where they lived until Guy's death in the mid-eighties. I was aware of Mule offspring graduating from Stissing Mountain High School and I was glad that the final chapter of his life story was a happy one.

After Guy's flight, the house was lacking its most colorful tenant but his room was filled with a variety of short term residents. One was actually a trio of Puerto Rican men who were working at a local business. The owner of Red Cap cleaners that was just beyond the playground on Smith Street persuaded Tillie to take the three for a week until he could find a more suitable situation. The men smiled and spoke broken English and told me they would teach me some Spanish. After work and coming back from the diner at Clinton Square, they liked to sit on our front porch where we had several rocking chairs. I would sit on the stairs and listen to them talk and laugh among themselves. A few words in their native tongue stood out clearly and I would try to repeat them to myself. I never really picked up much but it may have been their personalities or the fact that they had come from far away that I became interested in Spanish and took it throughout high school.

After that, a number of faceless short-term renters passed through the front door to trudge the three flights to Guy's old room. When the room was empty, I climbed to visit the empty room, to lie on the bare mattress surrounded by the gray walls to think of Guy and his new life. That soon became depressing, however, and after a period, I hardly ever went back to his room, for that was what it would be forever.

The second room on the third floor was the cell like bedroom of Art Ellsworth who drove an ambulance for Vassar Hospital. I have no idea how he had ended up at our house for the hospital was all the way down town, a distance of perhaps five miles. In those days people walked without complaint and so did Art. When he first arrived to rent sleeping quarters, Tillie welcomed him after the interview which revealed his occupation. I heard her tell my mother that Art had psoriasis which led me to the dictionary and an initial reaction which was to avoid him for fear it was contagious.

It was a five block walk to Main Street but we could always get a bus to go downtown to the movie theaters and another six or seven long blocks to get to the hospital. Art never seemed to mind the walk for he never complained to us. He was a reserved man who when prompted by Tillie would give some details about this or that accident that we had read about in the Journal. He was there at car crashes, fires and the aftermath of violence, which was sometimes a stabbing in the black neighborhood downtown. Tillie was a fire chaser. Once we heard the fire whistles we counted the number and went to a chart behind one of the kitchen cabinets to find the neighborhood and Tillie and I would follow. On some of those adventures, we saw Art sitting in his white ambulance or waiting outside with other men in white poised to pick up the injured.

If Art encountered me on arriving home, on the porch or in the hall, he would smile and pat me on the head until I was around ten and then he began to give me paperback books. He recognized that I had an interest in reading and having a small collection of detective and western novels, he began to pass them on. Since my mother said that Vincent had liked Zane Gray, when Art passed on a paperback, I attempted to read it as quickly as possible so as to show both my interest and seek the father that I didn't know.

Although he slept in the room next to Guy, he was as different as night and day. When I made my "secret agent" calls to Guy's room, I was never tempted to "spy" on Art. He was a nice man in a different way from Guy. He was private and would stop and say a few words to me, a kid, or my mother but he seemed to ask no more. When he left us after a couple years, we thought that he had met a woman and my mother was happy for him. Once, when I was out on an adventure with my friend Al Montalto, his ambulance was stopped at a light and he waved at me. And that was Art. He came to us quietly and left as quietly.

The last room on the third floor was a small bedroom which served as a storehouse of things Tillie or my Mother couldn't bear to part with. The inventory included old recording cylinders, postcards, birthday cards, dresses and dress patterns, numerous boxes of buttons, knitting yarn, needles, parts of sewing machines, and directions how to sew and mend. There were shoe boxes containing old shoes as well as old baby shoes. There were piles of old Look and Life magazines as well as pulp paperbacks- Ellery Queen, westerns and flowery covered romances. It was here that I spent some of my reclusive afternoons on snow days from school, while my mother was at one of her jobs. I sat on one of the piles and read old magazines, or ran my fingers through the buttons. I looked for forgotten treasure but never had any luck.

Frank Babcock was a third man who lived with us for several years, in fact he at times fancied himself a part of the family. He rented the middle room on the first floor. The front room was a bedroom but became a living room after my mother decided to move the TV from what was in fact the dining room. Frank was sandwiched between the two. Sometimes he would join us for evening television. He was without close family and so on Sunday when my mother would make a traditional meal, the aromas wafted into Frank's room. He was not reluctant to suggest to her that he was doing nothing on Sunday and so she sympathized with his loneliness and he would unlock the door between the two rooms and join us.

He flirted with Mom. It may have started as a seduction to get an invitation to join us but it got to a point that Mom feared he was looking for another wife. He would attempt to touch her at times, only a hand or a shoulder but I could see him approaching a hug. Although he was probably twenty years older, she was cautiously flattered. After all, the presence of Tillie warded off other men.

My two brothers gave him little attention, but since I was the youngest, I was often around and saw him as a grandfather figure. But unlike my own grandfather, Frank became the definitive curmudgeon. There were many things he didn't like: his old employer, his late wife, blacks, Jews and most politicians. This and the fact that he smoked cigars caused him to aggravate us increasingly through the years until my mother told him he would have to move. His demeanor turned dark; "his feathers were so ruffled" in my mother's words.

She made a point, it seemed to me, to be working at the cleaners on the day that the taxi came to pick Frank up. He packed and met the taxi as it sounded its horn. I don't think he looked back. As time went by, he was one of many who passed through our house and never returned. We heard that he had taken an apartment downtown but did not stay long. Perhaps he returned to Catskill where some of his family may still have been. Life at the rooming house had many 'perhaps' situations.

While Tillie avoided renting to women, because she thought they were "trouble" there was one special woman who stayed in the front room, which was to be my bedroom after college. This was a room with a single metal framed bed, a formica metal legged kitchen table in the corner under the windows from where you could see the traffic light at Mansion and Bemont, a mantel piece over a faux fireplace and a small gas top where one could warm up soup or water for tea or coffee.

Our minister of Washington St. Methodist church rang the doorbell one day and introduced us to Rosemary Woodruff. Her mother back in Portland, Oregon had written him a letter asking him to help find her way to a safe house and nice family where she could rent while living near Rollie, her husband who worked for the army and was stationed at West Point some fifty miles away. Rosemary was different. Her innocent charm took us all in. My mother thought she looked like Jean Crane, the movie actress. I thought she was simply beautiful.

The consensus immediately was that she was "sweet." I realized some time later that I had, like a cold, caught my first crush. She had explained to Tillie that her husband Rollie would only visit when he could because his job at West Point required that he not be distracted by family. And so it was some time until we were to meet her him.

Until that time, she often ate dinner with us. She would sit and talk to my mother while mom was doing kitchen chores. She became the daughter that my mother never had. The old kitchen with its soapstone sinks, wringer dishwasher and formica table spelled home to us and to Marion. Sometimes she would sit on the back porch to watch me play with my dog, Terry. When I tried to sit next to her every night, I think my mother realized that I was smitten.

Sometime within the first month of her stay with us, Rollie appeared. He was a tall, dashing fellow with a crew cut hidden under his army cap. He was extremely polite with my mother and grandmother at dinner and smiled broadly when Rosemary put her arm around me in way of introduction. She had been with us for a few months when Rollie and she announced upon his arrival for a weekend visit that Rosemary was pregnant. At dinner I quietly listened to the adults talk and answered the perfunctory question on school and sports. After dinner, Rosemary offered to help with the dishes but my mother encouraged the couple to retire to the TV room and simply said, "I have Richard to dry." I quietly complied and while I had many questions about their announcement, they went unasked rather than risk awkwardness; I would work with a dishtowel until it was wet and the dinner dishes were all piled up on the kitchen table.

By the time I got to the TV room, Rollie and Rosemary were sitting, his arm over her shoulder and I imagined them kissing until interrupted by my arrival. When they excused themselves to go upstairs to bed, I flushed with embarrassment at my thoughts. Rollie visited several times over that year and consequently, he too grew on all of us. We all looked forward to his next visit.

Time passed with Marion, gradually wearing maternity outfits to accompany my mother to a store or to Sunday church. Rollie returned that next spring roaring up Mansion St. on a Harley, wearing the cadet uniform of West Point. Married secretly against academy rules, he decided to confess to the administration and resign when the birth of the baby got closer. This was his last ride up the Hudson Valley, for soon his possessions arrived along with a small truck in which to put the motorcycle and they would return to Oregon where their daughter, Marcia would be born and they were to live with family. I was flattened by the loss.

I was very quiet as they made their last visit, loaded their car and began their goodbyes. We stood in the hallway to see them off but pretending that he had forgotten something Rollie went out to the car and returned with his West Point dress uniform, complete with helmet. "Would you like this?" he asked me; my mouth dropped at this offer. This scene sounds like it could be taken from a 1950 movie. The Long Gray Line was a TV favorite and I frequently followed the sporting events of "the Black Knights of the Hudson" in The Daily News. Rosemary smiled and hugged me before mounting the step of the truck. As they drove away, we all waved and my mother got misty at the loss of her surrogate daughter. I kept the uniform in my small room until it was consigned to the cedar closet in order to keep it safe from moths. I kept Rosemary in my secret thoughts until the time when I began to take the girls in my class seriously and made my first adolescent attempts to be charming with the opposite sex.

The oldest denizen of the front bedroom was Mr. Leopold. A little Jewish man who must have come to us by way of Mom's employer, Sadie Taub. Rooming next to the bathroom, was an advantage to a man his age because he could exit his room and be the first in the morning and simply open his door to step up to enter. The door had a frosted glass pane and whenever it was occupied the door would glow from the pull chain light within. My mother would take me up for my bath until I was perhaps seven or eight, fill the tub and leave me to the task. After a half hour she would return to check that I had cleaned all parts and hold the towel ready as I climbed out of the high, claw footed tub of another era.

The routine was broken by a major event- Mr. Leopold's death. One morning, other roomers complained about the door to the bathroom being locked and the workings of the house and their needs in trouble. After no response was heard from the bathroom, the police were called. I hurried to the front hall to see two strapping uniformed men marching up the stairs followed soon by the ambulance crew. Tillie was home, so she also attended the removal of the bathroom door all the time chatting with the cops who she knew from the "joints" she attended. I slipped up to the top step to get a better view as they lifted the door off the hinges. I then could see the naked leg of Mr. Leopold; the rest of his body was lying near the toilet.

The ambulance crew removed the body down the stairs to the waiting ambulance and the officers hung the bathroom door back on its hinges. His belonging were removed the next day and donated to the city mission. And while Mr. Leopold was gone, for several years I felt that his ghost was with me as I sat in the old bathtub. I would welcome my mother's checking on me for some time.

Jean and George Nader were next to stay in the front bedroom. George was a short smiling Syrian who was probably older when he met and married his wife. He worked at odd jobs but most often at a cleaners, pressing and ironing on the large steam equipment of the day. Jean was quite rural in mentality and while not homely was very plain, if not funny, in feature. It would be years until they had kids and so Jeannie at times took me under her wing. When Aunt Dot, as she called her, was working or eating at church, the Naders would treat me to something: a ride, ice cream or even the County Fair. In the summer, they would come to Copake Lake with my Mother and brother. George would fish and Jean would swim and it was once after swimming that her bathing suit slipped and I saw my first female breast. She actually apologized and offered the thought that I really didn't have to reveal the incident to Dottie. I promised our secret would be between us and remained both amazed and amused by the incident. I was nine and very much in the misty days of childhood.

The second woman to have the front room was Patty Schroeder, Jean's cousin.

Pat's Irish mother had died and her father was a rough Teutonic German immigrant who lived in New York city with her brother, Willie. Her father was a cook at a restaurant and must have kept long hours. He sent Patty to live with her grandmother in Pleasant Valley and she soon had a job as a telephone operator in Poughkeepsie. As Jean and George moved out, Patty on Jean's recommendation moved in. She could walk to work and escape from the strong rules of her family. Fate had it that soon, my brother Bob was released from the Air Force and picked up a job as a meat cutter at the nearby Bull Market with Guy Mule. Thus, they met. Bob fell for the petite cute Irish lass and they dated. Some summer nights I would run over to the school yard and looking up to her room could spy on them necking.

It wasn't a long courtship but one memory that I have is of the night that Patty and Jean, after some festivities impulsively bounded the back stairs, to tuck me in, although I was at least ten. Her visiting father followed and was enraged that his daughter would enter the men's bedroom and had to be calmed down by my mother. It was then that I realized what stress Pat must have experienced growing up with a father who after a few drinks would spew such anger. She carried that stress all her life.

Soon after, their wedding was held in Pleasant Valley at the Catholic church. My brother left Mansion Street for good and for the next ten years he and his growing family would only visit.

The front hallway which led to all life in 300 is an unforgettable part of the house. Not welcoming, it rather funneled people in and to their rooms. A cedar chest sat on the right before the stairs. Papers and mail rested on top until picked up by the person for whom it was intended. Underneath is where I stowed the stolen lifesavers from Tucker's store that the kid on the corner, George has pushed me to heist.

In the hall, I rolled out my linoleum bowling alley and knocked over plastic pins. Here, roomers would wait for their rides. And here, when I was a young teen, an intruder lurked only to be scared away by my mother.

Looking into the hallway through the beveled window of the front door, one saw a funereal light. Only on entering did the light from the converted gas sconce grow brighter. Still it failed to reach up the long staircase or to the end of the corridor and the doors of our family's rooms. Once acclimated to the dim light, the paisley pattern of the wallpaper and the muted gold of the old, worn wall to wall carpet became more evident. On sunny days a colored light came from the stained glass window at the top of the stairs. On summer days it swung open and the upper hall was brightened. Otherwise a church like light fell on the upper landing. I crept up this long staircase as a kid sneaking to Guy's room. As a college kid I climbed on all fours so as to hide the late hour from my mother.

The last of the roomers we had rented the front room of the house. Later it was to be a TV room, separated from Frank's room by large pocket doors made of beautiful oak. The old metal bed sat directly in front of these doors. Add a bureau and an easy chair, an old misshapened stuffed chair and a once elegant horsehair sofa with scrolled arms like the sofas that Cleopatra would recline on. The only renters that I can recall were Ralph Tucker and his son.

Mr. Tucker and son, who I will call Ralphie, owned one of the two grocery stores on the corner of Smith St., down the block. They slept at 300 Mansion for only a short time while getting established in the business and before they found a place for Mrs. Tucker and the rest of the family to reside. They were moving from Kingston and hoped to make it in a small business after Mr. Tucker had spent several years with Grand Union. He had taken over Skinner's which had been such a part of my youth. Mr. Tucker was nice enough, but seventeen year old Ralphie was a budding sexual miscreant. Not only did he show me racy magazines that he hid from his father but he maintained that he had experience with women. Much younger than he, I listened to his tales in awe but without much understanding. I was probably intimidated by his size and age, but I recall not liking him. When he showed me a foil wrapped condom and told me that he had to wear it when a girl sat on his lap, I passed the story on to my brother Don.

The next thing I knew Don had spoken to him and after that Ralphie had nothing to do with me.

In my later teenage years my mother decided to not rent the front room and make it the TV room. This was a great development for me because here I could invite a friend to watch the snowy picture of our RCA with rabbit ears and talk out of range of my mother. At seventeen probably, I invited a series of girls to watch TV and after saying hello to my Mother we would be left alone, only to be interrupted by her offer of brownies she had just baked or by the offer of a bowl of popcorn.

After I attended Dutchess Community College, I left home for Syracuse. This was slightly traumatic for suddenly I would be further from home than I had ever been. I had been to New York City a handful of times, and New Jersey once or twice on the Hudson River Day Liner with Mom and her friend. Syracuse was 250 miles away and Mom didn't fly, not that flying was an option, since she was phobic and my brother got agida at the thought of a long drive.

They ventured to Albany, to the theater to see Englebert Humperdink, or Dolly Parton or Lake George for an overnight, but never further.

They loved being home. For a time before they sold the house to a young family, Mom gave me the upstairs bedroom next to the bathroom where so many people had lived for a brief time. I no longer would share with my brother. This was my room when my future wife visited where she was able to experience my humble roots. I chose not to tell her about Mr. Leopold's ghost. The view of the elementary school as well as the traffic light at the corner and shared bathroom were foreign to her own quiet suburban home and was enough for her to think twice about staying long at 300.

I soon, however, left to share a house in the college town of New Paltz where I could relish my independence. On a road trip, I called to check in, as I always did and Mom made the announcement that they were moving! I was stunned. When I returned and visited the apartment that they had moved to I learned that my coronet and West Point jacket had been given away and many of my childhood "valuables" had been left with the house. Pep, the rocking horse, and some antique toys made it on the moving truck. My baseball cards were still in the closet.

Had I left a 1952 Mantle there or just dreamt it? Still I make that a part of the many reflections on my childhood home. After 60 years, dreams mix with memories to fill the blank spots that passing time has created. I once drove by the old house on a visit to Poughkeepsie to see if 300 was still there. It stands there still but has been aged by years of neglect. Nevertheless, the house and the people who are a part of my memory remain untouched by time..

Dorothy's Words

Papa was handsome; that I remember. He left when I was three to find work in Connecticut in 1916, because work was not easy to find. He wrote me cards and sent me a teddy bear on one of my birthdays. When he finally returned, he divorced Mama and had already started a second family. George, who grew up as my brother was in fact the son of Papa's first marriage. He did appear on occasion to take us out for a soda at Smith Brother's Restaurant. As years passed, he stopped coming altogether. A card with a dollar came from Connecticut until I was a teenager. I stopped missing him then and as I grew I stopped blaming him. He didn't leave just me. For after all, Mama was quite a rip!

Mildred Farrell and I played dolls at her house where there was a pet parrot, Polly. Polly would squawk as Mildred played the piano. We would all laugh. But I was seven and when Polly was allowed to fly around the house, I became afraid he would land on my head and pull out my hair. I began to have nightmares of running from Polly. I pleaded with Mildred not to free him from his cage, but she only laughed. In my 70's I would take the train to visit my son. My granddaughter had a parakeet; when she took him out of his cage, it all came back. Only when I put my hand on top of my head and stepped quickly out of the room did they understand.

How did I meet Vincent? One Saturday, I put on my weekend dress, one too good to wear in the coat factory, and went to visit my girlfriend May who had recently married an auto mechanic who was built like a gorilla and was slightly cross eyed. May was delighted to tell me that her husband's youngest brother was also coming and winked. I cringed to think what he would look like. When he knocked and stepped into the apartment, my body relaxed for he didn't look at all like Clarence. He was much taller with a long but handsome face; when he smiled, I felt my face light up. Behind him, May was winking again.

The Sunday telephone call: "Hi Mom, it's Rich."
"Well Richard. Where have you been now?'
"We just got back from Boston and then Concord where Hawthorne's homes are."

"Oh I went there on a Y trip with Sadie, who, well you know how fat she is, got stuck in the ladies room. The Guide had to unlock the door so that I could go in pry her out."

"Oh Mom- not a pretty picture!'

"We laughed the whole way back on the bus about it. Olga told us to be quiet which only made us laugh harder!.She wouldn't know shit from Shinola, that old biddy!"

At Victory Lake Nursing Home, Mom sits slumped in a wheelchair with ten other "easy riders."

A large Jamaican nurses' aide comes by and chirrups, "How's my Dorothy today?" My Mom looks up through glaucoma glazed eyes and seems to see her and nods her head. The aide continued to stroll down the hall and Mom says, " Maria's sweet. She likes me because I'm one of the few who hasn't lost my marbles! She gives me my bath." She smiles weakly and gives a palsied nod as if to reaffirm that Maria is indeed sweet.

Victory Lake

A panorama of chiseled faces, sculpted by time.

    Not Mt. Rushmore, but more real, more noble.

Carved and wrought by pain, and etched by memories.

    They are a large collection of untold stories only shared with unseen spirits and friends

long gone.

    Tales of family and friends now past, of lovers lost and school mates missed.

A game show on the t.v. hums unnoticed by most, a night light in the oncoming dusk.

    Some fall in and out of sleep, others stare at the unseeable.

They wait, many like mom in a wheelchair, ready to go somewhere.

    As if they're sharing time on a train station platform,

Waiting for the last local that will make a final stop

    Where only shadows wait to welcome them, to their hometowns.

Sunset and Evening Star

My Mother's eyes darken with each passing year;

> An eternal eclipse awaits the day to cross her face and leave her without light.

Then only sights of long ago will stay.

> All the dead who have passed her by.

The gardens that she loved, the stories that she read, the sights of travel.

> She'll return to childhood, a bow in her hair, a talking parrot, who sang while she played her piano, near its cage,

> Sit near her handsome papa who wrote her penciled letters after he left home.

In her memory's eye she'll scan the faces of her one room schoolhouse and read her primers

> Until dinner time and her chores are done.

She'll see the move from farm to city and the factory where she had to sew

> Coats and pocketbooks to help provide.

On weekends, she and a girlfriend would walk to the movies.

> The dreams of Errol Flynn or Tyrone Powers are still clear to her sightless eyes.

She sees once more the boy downstairs and plays a sweet coquette to his strong silence.

    How soon they shared a soda and listened to Benny Goodman or Harry James.

And smile still at the memory of his handsome face moving toward hers for that first kiss.

    They'll marry and she'll bear his sons, before losing him to fate and dark waters,

Sunday dinners, church services, pets and tenants of her rooming house.

    She calls up memories so clear that all the aged around her disappear.

Vincent

A moonless night on the lake; two men board a rowboat to cast their lines

    before the rising of the sun.

Two hundred feet from shore, and many miles from life, the old boat tips

    "Hold on!" one cries, but their heavy coats fill with water

    And draw them down to drown.

So my young father's life ends

And with him sinks so many moments that fathers are meant to have.

    From the shadows of lost years, he watches me.

We stand apart in the thin light of time past.

    His shady form is lean like mine and

He reaches out a finger across the many unshared years as if to touch a face

    He hardly knew.

I too reach out and come close to him, like God on the Sistine ceiling

    reaching to give life to man,

And look to know this phantom, who helped give me life,

    and in so doing know my own beginning.

Back at his home, his young wife turned in their bed to touch his place,

    Too soon cold.

The Sun's in My Heart

My mom would finish the dishes, comb her hair and grab her purse.

>We were off too see the new musical at the Bardavon.

A young widow and the youngest son, still too young to stay home alone.

>A three mile stroll down Main Street and a date with Gene Kelly.

A dancing singing Hollywood dream; for her, a way to slip away from memories.

>For me a boy meets girl tale.

A popcorn and coke and I was happier than Gene and his frolic about being in love.

>We smiled together in theater darkness, as Gene danced his way into "I'm happy again,"

"What a glorious feeling", mom sang.

> After the theater lights rose, I skipped from the theater, out to Market Street and over

the curb, in search of a puddle on a dry street.

> I tap danced while she hummed the melody from block to block.

Her voice trailed off as we rounded the corner toward our house.

> We were no longer in Paris.

I bounced up the stairs and into the dark hall of our rooming house.

> Our dreams of happily dancing and singing along the Seine would be put aside until

The next movie escape from Poughkeepsie and the past.

Sacred Stones: East Park, NY

The cold gray stones of the plot form a random pile beneath the leaking pines.

> Some have been shifted by roots or frosts of passing years.

All are spotted by the green mold of the graveyard.

> Here my ancestors rest from life,

Some I know only by black and white box camera moments

> Handed down to me in attempts to hold on to time.

They dropped off the family tree like fallen leaves, season after season.

> I am the last leaf, spinning by a stem
>
>> Hanging on.

Sitting next to tombstones is the quietest of times.

> The hush of old marble, mute witnesses of death.

A solemn ten foot hedge shelters those who sleep here from the

> Traffic noise of passing cars, just feet away from the never moving monuments.

Outside the wall, life speeds by.

> Here only ancient silence, and a season of falling leaves.

A Winking Eye

The red numbers on the clock radio flash out a lighthouse like alert-

    6:00 a.m.!

The coffee pot turns on with a welcoming blip..blip.

    The red flicker of the gas fireplace adds to the early morning glow.

The house is still dark.

    I wake, roiled by dreams of once upon a time,

What was replaced by what is and shades of what could be.

    I slide from the sheets and comforting down

And smile at the sonorous breathing of my mate.

    She sleeps on, drawing in the warmth of our bed.

Like a thief, I steal away into the still dark hall and the gray light of early morn.

    The kitchen lights shock my eyes and as I stumble into the approaching day

The coffee aroma surrounds me and suddenly, I need that first sip

    And the familiar warm grip of the mug.

I squint again at the growing light that now fills the kitchen window

    And when I blink, the sun seems to wink back at me

As if to say, "between you and me, there's always hope in a new day."

P.O.

Thanks to my grandfather on my father's side I have always thought of myself as English. Sometimes I've been Dutch, sometimes Irish but after that my known ancestry fades. My mother swore that there was an a native American in her family tree. I like the idea but can't be certain. However, what I am certain of is it that my grandfather Walter, nicknamed P.O.P, hailed from Barrow-in- Furness, England.

He was a little man maybe five foot seven, but more stable and stronger than most, from years of hard work, All of his four sons were taller and of varying builds. My father,the youngest was a six footer. But in 1949 and 1950, P.O.P, as my family called him seemed not much taller than I.

When he came from Michigan, where he lived with Uncle Roy, to spend Christmas with us, our house changed. He made the train ride ever since the untimely death of my father in 1946. Pipe and cigar smoke. The aroma of pipe tobacco filled the rooms of our old Victorian house: the cigars were relegated to the front porch, no matter how cold, where it would not irritate my mother. It was the pipe that filled me with its blue smoke as I hid behind a large reclining chair in the sitting room where I decided to try out this adult entertainment. As I puffed my way into a dazed state, a cloud of smoke gave away my hiding spot to my mother as she passed by. She only said, "I hope you get good and sick." I didn't get sick, but I did have a cough and a mouth as dry as a wrinkled autumn leaf for the rest of the day.

A few years later, P.O. defended me after a foolish experiment. A neighbor who was three years older invited me to his house. With no parents home, he opened his father's liquor and proposed "sampling." He told me the next week that he wanted to see what effect it would have on me. While I naively choked several swigs, he faked it by putting his thumb over the bottle. Soon the room was spinning and my nature changed which alarmed him and he helped me out of the house and down the street, sat me on the porch, rang the doorbell and ran home. P.O. realized my state, steered me into the first bedroom which was my mother's. I flopped delirious on the bed.

When he left to get me a glass of water, I promptly threw up in the middle of her bed. A whisky smelling mess! As he began to clean it up as best he could, Mom arrived from her afternoon job and stood stunned in the doorway by the state of her ten year old. She fumed, demanded an explanation and stormed to the phone to call George's mother. When she returned, P.O said simply: "Mother here's your son" as he stood between us.

On his visits we played checkers or card games. He taught me how to play poker and rummy, and we bet a penny a hand. These were activities we could do, things my father might have done if he were alive. On occasion P.O. would listen to me read the pirate or frontier story that I had taken from the school library. We watched Ed Sullivan or I Love Lucy together. We shared Gunsmoke or Rifleman after dinner on our 24 inch T.V.

When Christmas finally came, he would take the chair by the fireplace wearing his long underwear and suspendered pants and light up his pipe. The smell of evergreen mixed with the aroma of Sir Walter Raleigh. One long black sock was hung the night before along with my stocking for Santa. The morning ceremony started with our checking the contents. His contained a couple of new handkerchiefs, a pack of cigars and in the toe, a lump of coal. To my delight, P.O.P had been bad again. Mine held things like a racecar, a miniature revolver and in the toe, an orange. Tradition!

Although he was uneducated in the academic way, he managed his world. He worked as a building laborer in England where as a youth, he had hot plaster spilled on his head and he lost the sight of one eye. He worked at farming on Uncle Roy's Palomino farm in Michigan where he mowed the hay and fed the animals. He never lived to find that I would be a teacher and a lover of the literature of England. Yet, I like to think that he had a poetic spirit about him, however so humble, for when I was ten he had me memorize the following lines which his father had passed to him in Barrow.

My father's dead
He's gone to rest
He left me all his riches.
A feather bed, a wooden leg and a pair of leather breeches.
A coffee pot without a snout
A teapot without an 'andle (his accent)
A tobacco box without a lid
And half a frosty candle.

Around 1957, my grandfather returned to Dutchess County to bury his wife, Lillian, next to their youngest son, my father in the family plot in Hyde Park. Grandma Holt had an unsmiling pioneer look to her as though unhappy or not well. She lived with diabetes and P.O.P gave her a nightly injection of insulin. Being her caretaker so long, perhaps both wore him down and maintained him for in only two years his body was put on the train to Poughkeepsie and he was interred with his wife and son.

Memory of a good, simple man stayed with me all of my life. I'm certain I inherited some of his nature. Many of my ex-students still recall me as a "good" guy. I tried to forget Leo Durocher's infamous line, "nice guys finish last." because I still feel ahead in the game. When I retired from the Niskayuna Town Board, a fellow councilman said of me that I had always been "one of the nicest guys." If that is part of my legacy I leave my grandchildren, so be it. With it I hope they have two other things. The first Is that I was a teacher and second, thanks to my grandfather, P.O.P I was always English.

The Old Cabin

The old cabin had been in the family since 1930. Metal roof, clapboard siding, wood frame windows that were weathered and skewed by time. Screens had been nailed on and instead of being replaced by aluminum, they were taken down and new screening stapled on. The inside hadn't been modernized either. Three small bedrooms separated by pine partitions, a bathroom with sink and mirror- the family washed in the lake and a kitchen where appliances never seemed to age. The living room was where they ate and played board games or one could simply rock in the old rocking chair with a coffee or beer, depending on the hour, and soak in the view of the lake below.

For years, there was no running water. As a kid, I would take the metal bucket from the kitchen, at my mother's request and walk down the road to the community well. It had been an early passage to be tall enough and strong enough to pump the gushing water and to carry it back to the kitchen for drinking and boiling for coffee. The privy was a typical country landmark. Most summer residents had one. Painted in matching colors with the house; its odor demanded a weekly sprinkling of lye. Once when its contents failed to deteriorate rapidly enough, my older brothers tipped it over, shoveled it out and trucked the load to the town dump.

Basic was the only word to describe Bingo, named for my grandmother's love of the game. It was bought with the $500 prize that she won one night at the Elks Club bingo hall. They all loved it but for me it was a special retreat from the black topped neighborhood playground at home. It was a safe place for a kid to roam, to discover and to grow up. My brother Don taught me to fish and take the rowboat out on the lake. He gave me my his first sips of beer behind our mother's back. It was Don who showed me my first pin-up of a pretty, scantily clothed girl that was hidden under his mattress.

It was here that I watched my brothers interact with girls and other high school friends. I was the kid brother who would sit on the dock, as the teenagers would dive off the deep end, laugh, and chase each other in the water. Older girls noticed me by teasing me and ruffling my hair.

It is a page in my story.

Bingo

It's fall on Copake Lake.

> the view of the water is a cracked landscape of leafless trees.

Out there my father died so long ago

> His cries for help lost in the dark, early morning air

And he was lost forever in the dark waters.

> I've returned to the old family retreat to check it before the winter.

Those who loved it more than I have died; since 1945, our summer place

> bought with Gram's winnings from a bingo game

Once full of life, now an almost abandoned shanty.

> With cautious steps, I enter this summer home of my youth.

A shell of memories now; only dust and knicknacks survive.

> It smells as if it has been closed up a century.

Old voices buried in the dust and lost in the webbed gray carpet

> Call out to be vacuumed, bagged and discarded

Along with the tracks of mice.

> Outside the honks of geese resound off the still face of the lake.

They break the silence of ghosts who once upon a time rocked in the now silent chairs.

> Old prints that have hung forever seem one with the wall:

Jesus. Bing Crosby and Ben Hogan stare at me, as if I am a trespasser.

> A shower of memories rain down on me and soon turns to a downpour.

I'm suddenly soaked in flashbacks.

> As I turn to leave, I see my mother in her house dress bent over the bucket of well water ready to boil the potatoes for salad.

> A chill runs through me, and I step outside to breathe the cool autumn air

And flee the past.

Sons

In you, my son, I have grown small again

    Allowed to rediscover things lost to ears and touch-

The crunching of autumn leaves

The sounds of creatures both large and small

A playground world in which to run and hide.

I grip a book and beer can, symbols of age, my reign.

    In balance with your truck and shovel, we play out our roles.

My book, a tale of sad despondent souls are strangers to your kingdom.

I sip my beer and watch you, to heal the pain of my fictional world.

    And in you a different new world I see-

One to be dug up and piled in a Tonka truck

    To dump and fill imagined pot holes.

To smooth the road from child to man,

    from son to father.

Lleyton 2015

I've watched you grow

    A sapling of a boy.

Slow to bloom, but filled with energy to run and climb.

    With a boyish zest for trucks and planes,

For legos with which you build the future.

    Boy games celebrated with a whoop and holler!

You relish the sand of the beach or the dirt of a playground,

    There for you to dig and move and shape new worlds.

You tease your sister until she screams, and you love her in a headlock

    A son for my son, a boy for my boy,

A joy to watch you playing your role.

To Sara 1975

A three foot gamboler who prances through the yard,

    Her fenced in universe.

Where bouncing horse, swingset, ball, and a kiddie pool fill-up her world.

    She lifts a five inch sneakered foot to vault a rock, a pipe, a leaf

And lands softly in the flower bed.

    A wrinkled nose snorts at the petals of a red flower

Which in turn, perhaps, inhales the perfume of a child.

To Lucie 2015

A fairy sprite who flies before my eyes

    An Ariel who points the way to magic

For grownups who have lost the knack.

    There are dinos good and bad out there,

Who tromp around the pillow castles built from the wreckage of the couch.

    Sometimes on the way to school, a purple whale appears in the river

Named Sesame whose eyelashes splash on the water's face.

    Later like a young fawn she runs the green lawns of Boston or Opa's house.'

She gallops the beaches of the Cape or Westport or Turks

    And like her Mom before her, she is a natural on the bars and trails of playgrounds.

Part monkey, all little kid.

    "I'm not an aminul," she'll say "I'm Lucy, I'm a girl!"

Cora at 3

Her impish smile disarms attempts to restrain her.

> She brushes back her golden locks with the back of her hand,

And with a wiggling run escapes, her arms swaying in time to her pony like gallop.

> A fairy sprite that could have danced after Will's Titania into the mythical forest.

Her magic is in her smile and the wave of her imaginary wand that can turn her brother into a

> good monster.

Her eyes tell the story, often widening in delight.

> She's Disney's Elsa the princess, or so her dress from "Frozen" says.

She plays at being a child but shows her stuff against the boy who would take her lightly.

> And is quick to say no when challenged.

But then again,

She melts in tears in her father's arms when needing a hug,

> Like future lovers will melt in her's.

The Greyhound Station 1969

Travelers and derelicts fill the room waiting

> In cloudy ashtray gloom until outside the bus appears.

It looms over the lot like some awful animal,

> as people file in shuffling gait toward the stairs to reappear in

Dirty, streaked, eye like windows of the beast that has passed through the gray decaying

> towns of industrial America.

On blackened snow filled streets they'll ride toward thruways and beyond

> To be released like prisoners paroled into another life

Away from this dirty, diesel crossroads.

> Now almost abandoned, the station sits quiet

Marked by squalid floors of discarded newspapers

> And stubs and butts and footprints stained by mud and snow.

The tracks of those long gone.

Crouse College, S.U. 1977

The granite spires stand out against the cloudy skies

    Sentinels guarding the campus far below.

Over University and Irving Ave- past Comstock, and Genesee Streets

    The hourly knells wrap The Stadium in sound.

The bells of Crouse ring in the dreams of freshmen and take Alumni back to days of youth

    And promise.

Of hopes and expectations and the glory of each orange day spent on the Hill.

    A tradition tolling for S.U.

Ringing out their song eternal heard by students both here and gone.

    The streets below the hill smile at the familiar sound that rolls

Beyond the city, beyond the lake and over the hills of Onondaga.

Omniscience

If I could move between the seen and unseen I might know it all,

    But then again, who can understand that which we do not see?

Who can only trust in God or whatever Spirit we invoke

    To show us the invisible truths?

Thus on I plod without a plan, and find myself lost in a jungle of thoughts,

    No guide to lead me out.

    And still I try to guess that which is unguessable..

If only I could see what I cannot, would I shake my head in disbelief of life going on and on?

    Would I know how to trace my starting place until the finish?

If so I'd know which way to go, I'd know it all,

    I'd know it all.

All in Light

"It's easy if you try" John Lennon

I feel the weight of walls that sit heavily between people.

    The rift of color that sets white and black apart,

The word at home that proclaimed "they're different, keep away!"

    Poets and dreamers see a world made one, a community,

Being human, leaving a mark, a footprint on the earth.

    The shared experience of living taller than man-made walls.

Joy and suffering mixed into all our drinks,

    Happiness and pain sprinkled on all our food

No matter how humble or rich, no matter how hungry or full.

    Secure within or insecure without the ramparts of our doing.

Imagine each of us, a little world that spins, and spins like the planets,

    Half in darkness, half in light.

Imagine all in light.

    Imagine.

Fleeting

Like quicksilver, time slides away into strange shapes

> Spreads like a spill, into shining fingers reaching out on floors or tables,

Running finally into thin streams, thinning out until it almost disappears.

> "The sands of time" is worn out but apt as it pours from our cupped hands.

"Hold on" we say, a cry in the wind, a futile plea.

> Time finds the crack. so small, between our fingers and drops grain by grain

Until seconds become hours become days and then years,

> And we look away aghast.

Our hands now empty, our schemes and hopes have thinned,

> Until all we can grasp is ourselves

The Last Syllable.

1.

Days float, as if the stream of life will flow on and on.

> Over submerged objects, below the surface of consciousness.

Some days are droughts, when the stream's face withdraws to show once submerged

> Thoughts and feeling

Cast into the waters to sink so deep they drown.

2.

Life can be stopped up by regret.

> Past mistakes and misdirections stand in the way.

Words left unsaid, acts never done, hugs never shared

> Haunt like ghosts calling to be dispelled.

And so, I cannot dwell in a world unrealized.

> And fantasize how I would have spoke, what I could have done, how I would have kissed

If I were only able to turn back pages, cross out lines, insert some others

> And change the denouement of my story.

Life in Limbo

with apologies to Ulysses

Like a gentle tide on Long Island Sound

> I at times am in the bay and then again, I'm on the shore

When I'm not here, I'm there- but where is that?

> Between Heaven and Hell? Well, almost

But perhaps fearing one and seeking the other.

> I strive on, through a misty land of remembrance and an island of forget.

And so I write about my thoughts and build a bridge between then and now,

> Between if and only,
>
> > why? and why not?

I sail on a sea of paper and print around the isles of peril

> in search of the Lotus eaters

Shall I drug myself from past pain, to escape and fight again ?

> Or strive to keep sharp my wits, to seek, to find and not to yield.

October Drive 1980

Gold and green leaves shine in the autumn sun.

> Flashes of red and orange, like warning lights, guard the road's edge.

They blow by as a sign of the season, dislodged.

> To float through the air blow on and on and fall for the second time.

I speed past the woods

> Still, I glow in autumnal colors,

I spin amongst the trees, a human leaf.

Not frost laden yet, bearing news of winter,

> A harbinger of months and years to come.

Not in the fall of life I write,

> But in the heyday of my time,

A time to hold this moment in my mind.

> And draw on it as seasons pass

A time to love, to kick the leaves and see them piled up,

> Oh for a moment to be a child again, to jump into and bury myself within!

But accelerate I must through the seasons, and know the earth will turn again.

Eternal Sunrise

As it has done for centuries

Sunlight breaks the gray mood of the early morning on the Bay.

> Gentle waves rouse the sandy shore to life.

Good morning Brewster.

> The heralds of the air leave their roosts to announce their search for food.

They criss-cross the Cape, marking their way with cries,

> Leaving patterns like jets in an air war in the brightening sky.

Below, early morning walkers take their laps along the shoreline.

> In silence but for the rapping of a woodpecker, the squawking of crows and the crying gulls.

It's a world still damp from the evening mists.

> The birth of a new day,

The promise of yet another rising.

The Escape of Summer

It flirts with us, draws us outdoors and soon we fall in love with blue skies.

    Sometimes lost in sultry days and verdant, fertile growth, we live in the moment.

Too soon, our seasonal lover grows fickle and turns a cold shoulder.

    The hot breath of summer turns cool and the curtain of long days comes down too soon.

Sheets become blankets, iced drinks change to hot coffee and tea.

    The wine of the evening is changed to the scotch of a cold night.

We shift to wool or flannel, to ward off the chilly fingers of fall.

    And while we hope for a few warm days for a country ride, a last round of golf,

        a last rose in the garden,

Summer has fled.

    The house turns cold.

No ardor in the hot breath of the gas stove.

    No warming light at six but only the cool, dark air of October.

The windows stay black with night broken only by a neighbor's porch light,

    A lighthouse in an inky sea where a half moon sails.

Reluctant to wake up with my warm feet on the cold floor,

    I savor the last minutes under a warm blanket and imagine dozing in the sun.

Hot coffee awaits to warm my body but like a sad refrain,

    I'll rub my eyes and wonder where did it go?

Ode to PHS

Dawn peeks under the shade of my bedroom window

    And stirs me to remember -

Somewhere between two and four I've dreamt of high school days.

    An endless school-scape of teenagers of another time passing through halls to class.

Beautiful, plain, awkward or smooth

    They laugh, talk endlessly, some flirt some jostle.

A few pass silently to their next class in teen-age limbo

    where they likely will spend the rest of their lives.

What I retain are like snapshots in my dreams.

    Once color, then black and white and now with sepia tones

        photos of high school printed by nostalgia.

"The way we were" has led us to what we are,

    Lovers of yesterday and today, acceptors of tomorrow.

Owners of beginnings together and lives lived apart.

    Once a brave new world was ours filled to the brim with anticipation -

Just kids whose real beauty lay somewhere ahead,

    Some hopes deferred, some hopes attained.

And still, before sunrise, in early morning dreams,

    I leave my house to walk crosstown

        and walk down Forbus St

To the misty fields of P.H.S, and I feel my heart beating quicker.

Infatuation

An infectious laugh,

    A feminine guffaw.

She stands on the tee, gracefully posed over her ball.

    Her club swings perfectly straight back.

The shaft making her a part of an equilateral triangle.

    Her blonde hair down, eyes on the ball, she rises like a ballerina on her toes,

A quick rise and fall.

    A subtle wiggle of her well shaped bottom.

A quick windmill swing high over her baseball cap and connect!

    Her follow through spins her still narrow hips

Her slender legs twist toward the flight of her titleist.

    "Good swing!," I cry.

She turns to me and laughs, in response.

    A huggable golf partner is she!

A Last Round 1990

On a clear December morning, I walk the hushed fairways of Warwick,

> The cold quiet is broken at times by a distant leaf blower, happy to be still clearing

The last traces of November leaves.

> No trace of snow yet.

The only white, is my golf ball on the barren ground.

> The t-shot soars skyward, flying in the cool blue and disappears beyond the dogleg.

A rush of adrenalin warms me as I hike in its direction.

> The seven wood, a miracle for hackers, lofts the ball just off the green.

A Top-flight in flight.

> With my putter, I run the ball over the winter grass and it makes its way toward the flag.

Two feet: my cold face forces a stiff smile.

> The almost leafless trees, my only gallery, stand silently around the green

As I sink the putt for a par.

> The only applause is the rustling of the wind driven grass.

Playing Lahinch 1997

I drive off the first tee into a strong headwind,

> My ball seeks to lose itself in the deep grass of the green moonscape, dune filled fairway.

The first two holes lull me into the illusion that I can play Ireland.

> As we turned on the third I stagger in the gale off the Irish Sea

I grab my hat for dear life.

> I wait until my wind aided quiver over the ball subsides enough to swing.

The par threes almost greet me with an Irish smile. The game! Lad!

> A bogey has a beautiful sound.

The white breakers of the nearby sea draw my eye from the ball and it soares in a graceful

Slice joins the flight of the gulls and lands somewhere on the shell tattered beach.

Blind shots over and around grassy bluffs force our group to explore the gorse.

    Where's the ball now?

Goats munch on like gaelic lawn mowers never glancing at passing Americans.

    What's five lost balls and a lost hat compared to this?

Golf followed by the awaiting Guinness and stew or porter and chowder in front of the telly

    Surrounded by the music of Irish voices of the pub.

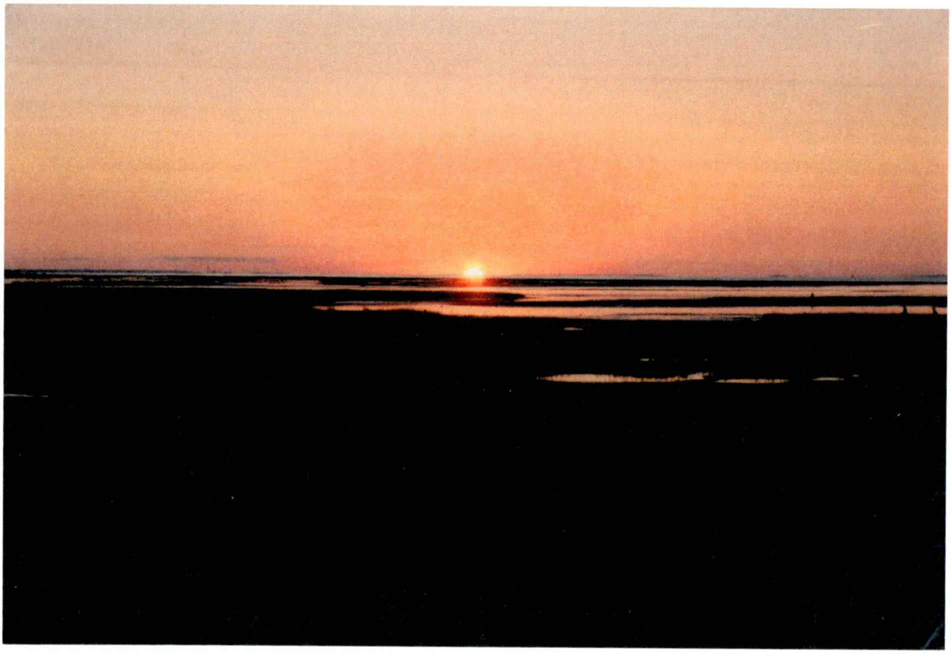

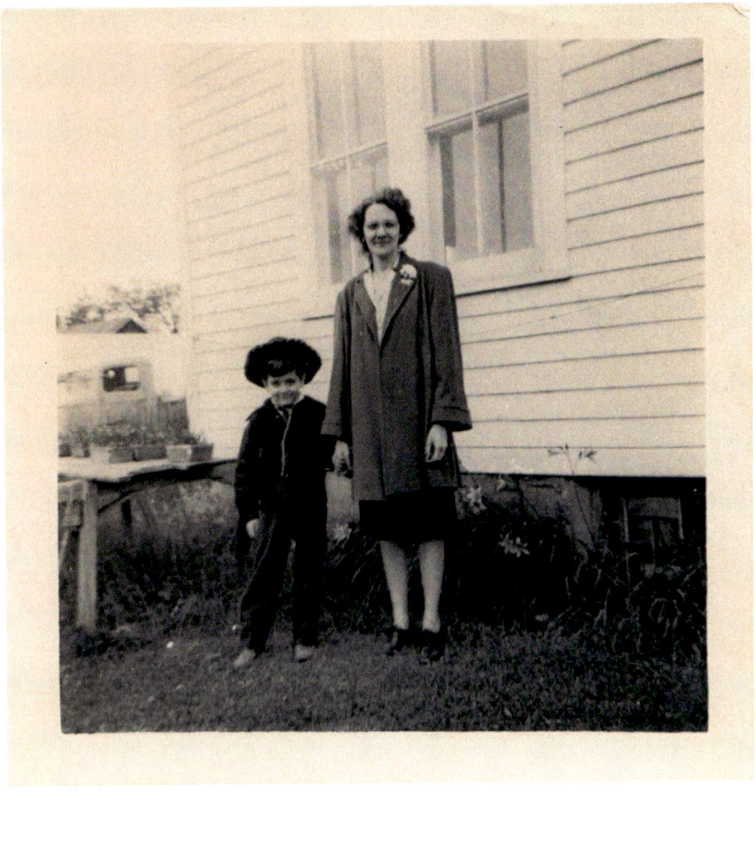

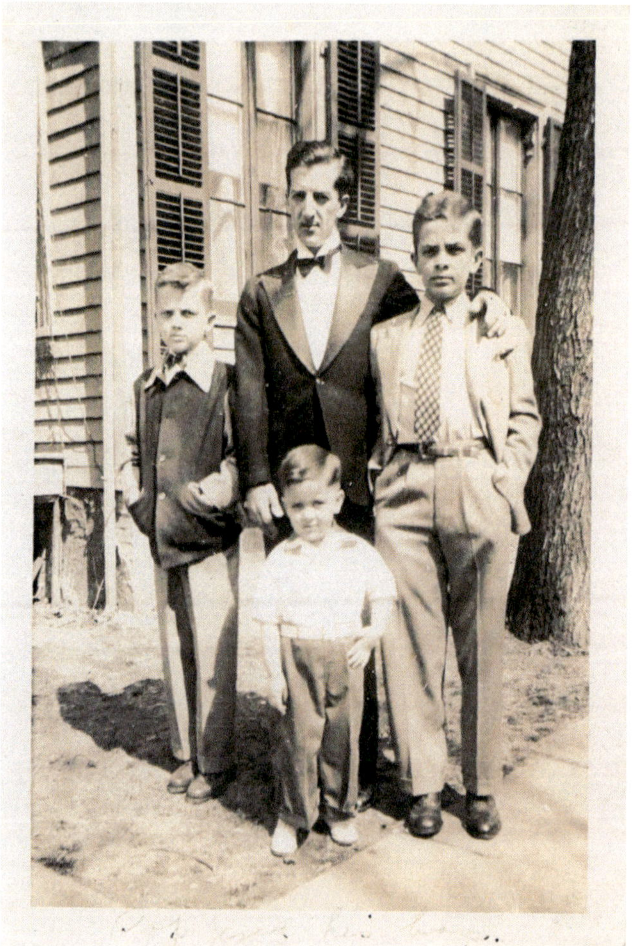

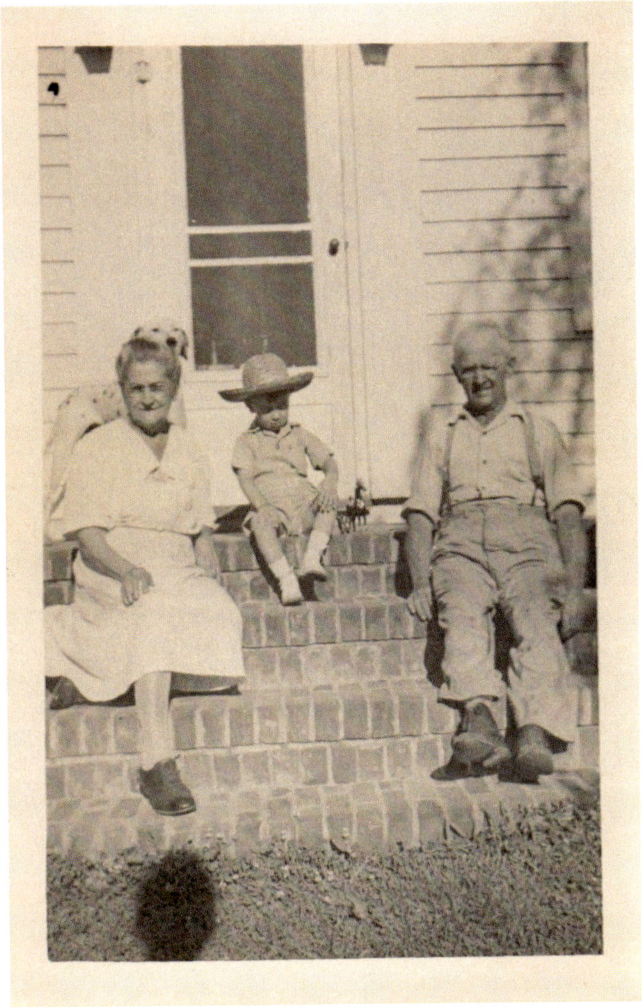

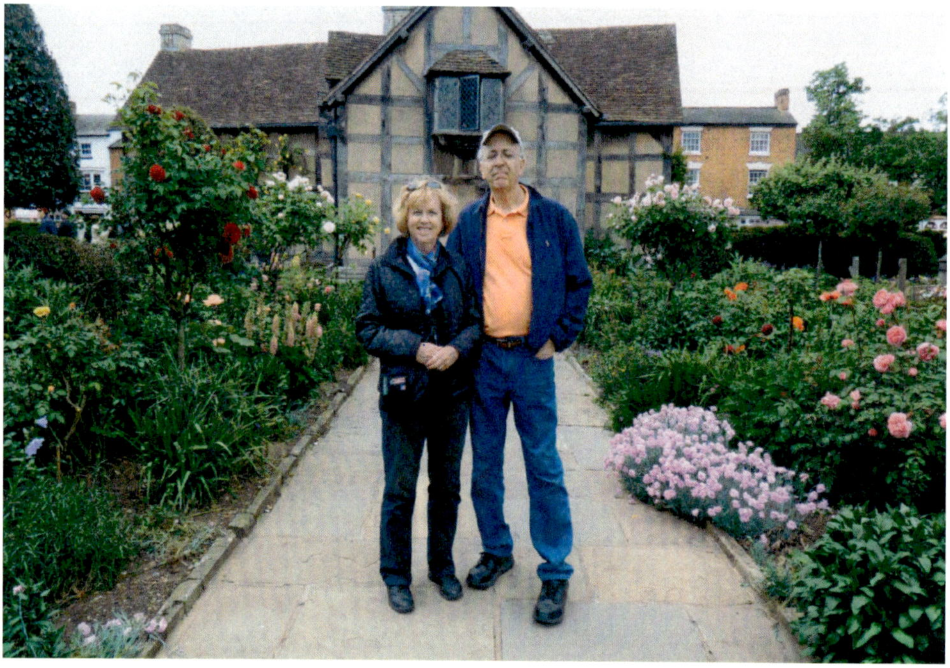

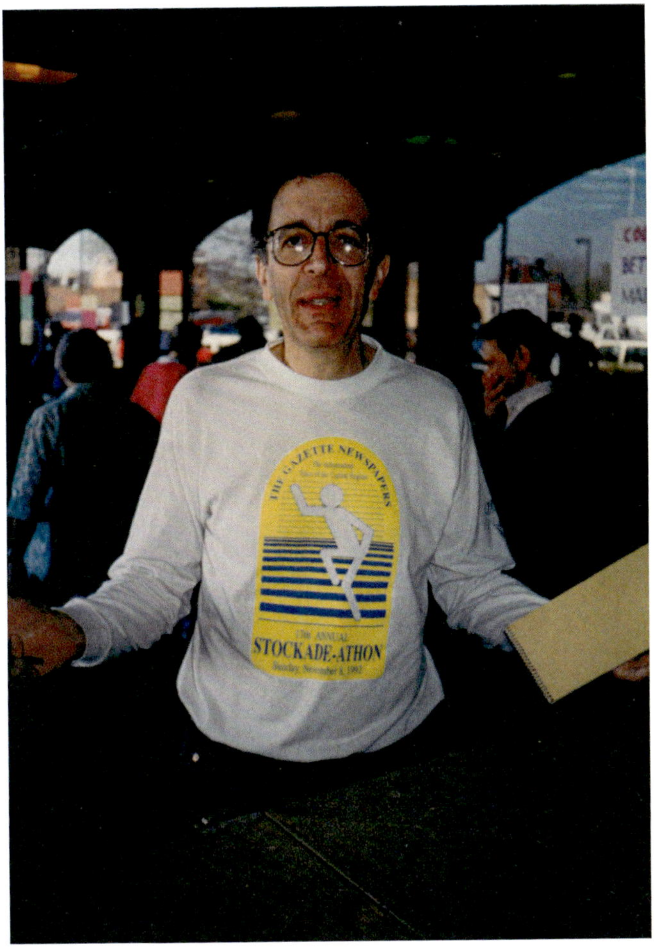
THE GAZETTE NEWSPAPERS
STOCKADE-ATHON

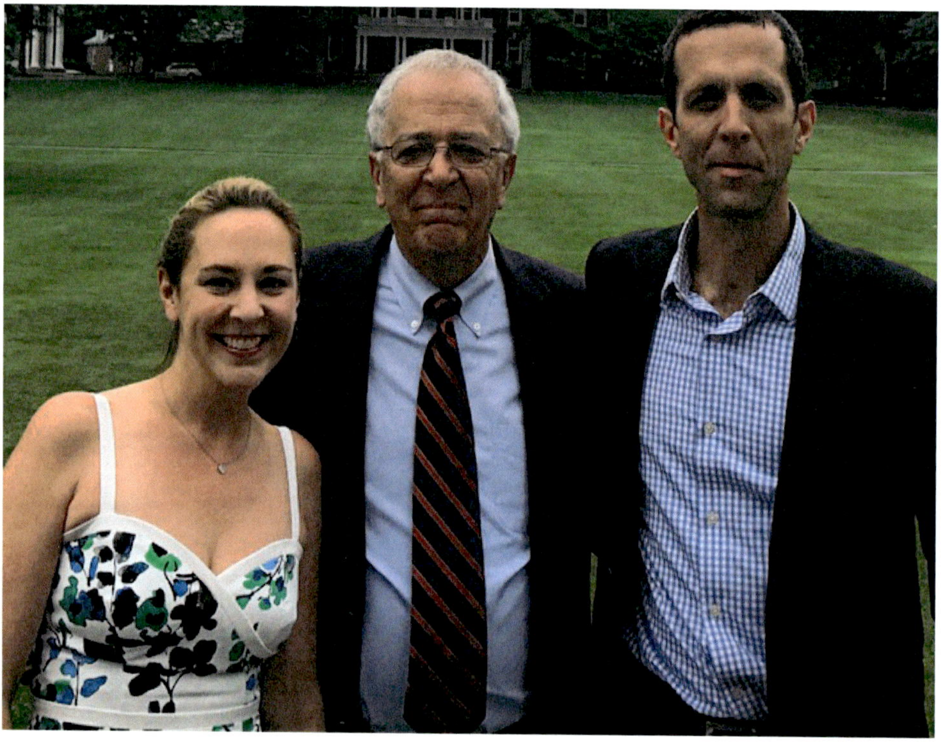

A Leaner

Cold blue skies and blinding late fall sun,

    Light up the fairway to make crisp all trees and bends.

Once or twice my shot rises and disappears into the glare.

    A partner helps with "you'll be ok with that"

Not wanting to look foolish I ask,"Right side?' and with a nod he saves me.

    I stagger off like Mr. Magoo.

And hope that I'm following the path of the ball.

    "More left!" he calls from the tall grass where he searches.

Soon I see a white spot ahead, sitting up in wait for my next shot.

    I turn as he swings fiercely into the bush and swears; at times such is life.

I mutter to myself as I approach, nine iron in hand and settle over the ball -

I think one..two..three and the club rises and falls- the titleist flies.

    Lost again in light, I hold my follow through and wonder:

"Live in hope, die in despair," my mother would say, and so must I.

    Resigned to fate, I begin my hike uphill to the green.

My game is one of discovery but

    how will I act when life becomes unplayable?

To lose the ball in water or sand, to be out of bounds and still respond.

    But as I step on the green, my ball peeks from between the side of the cup and leans on the

        Flag like an old friend.

To hole out on the 18th; a vision to last all winter.

Cafeteria Cutie 1989

She's draws on her straw with the insouciance of youth,

    A coy mistress with a milk carton.

Her long blond hair caresses her cheek and falls languidly on her shoulders.

    Her gently molded features neither smile nor frown at the life that swirls around her.

Shielded from the commoners, she shuffles the pages of the book before her.

    She nips the roast beef sandwich made in the auroral morning

By her discreet, careful Camelot hands.

    She pauses and her sculpted beauty breaks for a moment,

Pretending to acknowledge a passing boy.

    Gracefully she curls her legs cat-like under her

And gazes into the air, above the heads of all

    Seeking only distance from the every day crowd.

Teaching Dreams

It's been years since student essays filled my nights, red pen in hand and desk light in my eyes.

    A labor of love, or so I thought.

But still in dreams, I teach.

And students hang on my every word or smile at new understanding of the worlds

    Of Shakespeare, Wordsworth, Marquez, or Whitman.

My style like Letterman's, humour from movies, satire or just the news.

    I toss my sheets and roll in sleep when my adolescent's act their age.

Teach through humor and love of words- they'll get it.

Night visions of various classes return to me, some good others a freudian trip into

the teenage subconscious.

    When new to the classroom, I'd dream of flying through the halls on the fleet wings of Imagination.

    Daring to soar close to the sun.

But now my high school days and theirs mix, as my melted wings have sent me in spirals,

    descending closer and closer to earth.

Until I sink into a sea of memories.

A Tribute to Bob Williams

He was Sir Bob, or should have been.

    Knighted by Life itself.

A nobleman with feet in Pennsylvania, and soul in all the world.

    Courtly in manner, self taught in the finer things.

Particular as to what is correct, not a dictator but a mentor to students of all ages.

    What cheese and vintage were well married,

A scotch and where and when 'twas distilled was all quality and class,

    As was he.

Well traveled and well read in life's volumes,

    The rare and little known was his in witty twists and turns, in words or song.

A life long learner of weather and wind, of star and planet.

    And tongue in cheek, he'd share it with us all.

A second family so rare had he, led off by a mate, a counterpart, a compliment

    Both student and guide was she.

Together they had children three: a lass so sweet that found a home in Ireland,

    A sister, sexy, strong and smart; and last a lad with charm of both.

Sir Bob outlived a bullet from the war and fought the cancer to the last, with

    Wit and knowledge, a humor to live or die.

The world was bettered by his quest.

She Soars: to Linda Witkowski

From my window seat on the 747, I look down on miles of clouds

    Breaking under us, driven by the wind.

Some take shape with others, some fly as wisps through open space.

    The air, I know is freezing but rare, thin and special. Breathed by the gods.

I think of Linda, a spot of sunlight on a cloud shrouded day, a metaphor that

    Struck us with beauty and truth.

A beam of sunlight between the breaking clouds, making warm patterns

    On a cold earth.

I think of Linda at thirty thousand feet, rising above the small winged creatures, like us

    Coasting on the winds of words

To heights that only she and the greatest poets know.

    Where souls are lightened by the song of language,

We've been empowered by her touch and flung earthward at her loss.

    With her we shared the lofty heights and soared with angels.

A New Old Flame

A good loves never dies, but only fades.

> The fire of passion closed up by time, like fireplace doors restraining the last embers.

Memories of interlocking limbs, of never ending kisses, of the scents and tastes of romance

> Carried somewhere in the maze of memory, seen once again as in a dream, a lost fantasy

> That can live like a poem once memorized, whose lines and figures still float on high.

Sometimes they rhyme, sometimes they float in and out of the current of the mind.

> A life full of events and things has happened in other arms.

>> Even golden rings that lock two people in and old lovers out.

Two bodies in rhythm tell best of any loss to other loves that came and went

> Making the rhyming couplet of the past, a start rather than end.

The tale is revised when lips and tongues meet once again with a slipping together

> Where ecstasy becomes too mild a word.

When mouths and kisses spread to private parts of here and now,

> And then, and then hearts stop to rest from beating a rhythm never attempted by a line

of verse

> And waves consume us, yes.

Rediscovery

When the love of an old flame relights many miles and years later,

    The fire can still be ignited like the fuse of a lost explosive.

A once upon-a-time ardor, a conflagration of youth that burned almost out of control

    May now have become a candle to grace a romantic dinner.

Each meeting years ago was passion blinded by never ending kisses,

    Which left bruised lips and breathless moments.

Such heat seems chilled and lost forever, when two lives diverge and age

    Lives spent in the arms of others, now lost to death or separation.

A desire thought no longer on the map can drive a twilight two toward unplanned ecstasy.

    To a land thought lost, now rediscovered.

Where once we stopped, to only visit, no plans to stay.

    A love lost in the dust of time, but now uncovered.

With

Chance?

Life takes us in a variety of directions. Some are the result of choice, but many are the result of chance. Even if we feel in control and choose, we may not know where we are going until we get there. Shakespeare's Richard III said "if chance will have me king, then chance will crown me so." Looking back, I marvel how often chance crowned me. My choice of colleges, my profession of secondary teaching and most important to my life, my wife, Lisa.

After Poughkeepsie High School, I enrolled at Dutchess Community College. By chance I had two inspiring English professors; the first was Bill Heffernan who had also been on the basketball team at St. John's. I was on the bench for the DCC Blue Falcons and we could touch on poetry and ball, too. I had a new hero. The second was my British lit class. The Professor drew me into the Romantics and Victorians with a sophistication that I hadn't encountered. She was German and had an enchanting accent particularly in reading poetry. She brought out my best and when she left for a position at NYU she invited me to visit her when in the City. Although I regret not doing that, I saw the light and changed my major from engineering to liberal arts. Literature was to be my fate.

At the end of two years it was transfer time. I had become fast friends with Mike who was also a fellow P.H.S grad and was a much better student than I and so when he told me that he was considering the University of Buffalo and Syracuse University, I went along for the ride. I had a car, thanks to my brother, and so we were off to Central New York. After our campus tour and a sample of college life at the Orange bar, we continued on our trek west. But first we had to find a room for the night.

Serendipity stepped in. Somehow we were drawn to the home of Mrs. Treloar on the west side of the city. She and her husband, a retired gentleman who was an avid ham radio operator, took in SU parents and prospective Orange students in a B&B arrangement. Returning from the campus tour, we informed her that SU was impressive but maybe too large, and for me, too expensive. We were "shuffling off to Buffalo." Disappointed, she explained to us how her son had attended SU and all the family loved the university. She made us promise that on the way back we would stop and give the 'Cuse a second look. We did as we promised, and spent a second night with the Treloars. It was settled. If we hadn't found Mrs. T, we probably would have been trekking to Buffalo, which in those days got more snow than even Central NY. Thanks to her motherly advice, I've been Orange all my life.

74 | RICHARD HOLT

After I graduated, with an English degree, the next question was how to use it. Business school at SU or a Master's program at Albany. Not waiting for chance to step in, I began the program at UA. Not happy with my decision, I looked further, consulting Mike who was attending New Paltz State and found, by chance that his housemate had left and he might have to move home and commute. The trumpets of fortune were sounding (I had heard their clarion call before). I threw my clothes in a garbage bag, piled my paperbacks in boxes from the liquor store and took my VW south to the scenic village in the Mid-Hudson Valley, twenty miles from my mother and home. It was providence for there I met Dr. Sam Shaw whose passion for literature convinced me that I now was going in the right direction. The Education department's, Bob Boquist, was my mentor who guided me to student teach at Forbus Junior High in my old school district for Mr. Bob Corliss, father of a good friend by the same name. It was a fortuitous match and a colorful staff of devoted educators with whom to work.

When I finished at New Paltz, by chance Mr. Corliss needed an English teacher. While I hadn't planned on that age level it was an experience that I was to treasure forever. Mr. C was a father figure to me. He was a role model as an educator and family man as well. I learned much about life and myself from this chance opportunity.

My next chance occurrence came in the romantic realm. While I often fell in and out of love (for many reasons), there were few co-eds with whom I saw myself tripping down the primrose path of marriage. Put simply I was not ready, until the right one came along - song lyric material. Another factor was that my housemate, decided to jump into matrimony and I thought, "now there's where life should take us!" But who would it be?

My current flame was a beautiful, mercurial younger girl with whom I made great music for only a few beats in the long scale of things. Little did I know that she was seeking her identity and I wasn't to be a part of her orchestra.

She still seemed to be the one when I met Lisa in my room mates wedding. Lisa and the bride were close friends in their Catholic High days, and she was asked to be a bridesmaid. I, as the best man was expected to flirt with all bridesmaids and so I did my job.

They all were pretty on a pretty occassion, but Lisa in particular caught my eye. As planned, my flame of the month had come to Mechanicville the site of the festivities to pick me up and went to get the car for I had celebrated beyond the safe driving limit. As I passed the bridesmaids I detoured to bid adieu to the cute Miss McNamara and I was drawn to give her a more than friendly kiss. She later told me that she was shocked, but in addition I left her with a naughty joke. I hardly remember the joke but there was something in that chance kiss.

Not long after the bride and groom had returned from their honeymoon, my girlfriend of the month gave me a goodbye kiss of another sort and dropped me off on a corner in New Paltz, vowing to call. She never answered her phone after that. Her apartment looked empty from my passing car. And I finally had to admit to myself that I had been dropped off indeed. I had been dumped in the Shaungunk Mountains. I had been gunked as I dubbed it and stuck with memories of a beautiful long haired girl and two rather expensive tickets to see the Young Rascals, appearing in Albany. I bemoaned my state to my best friend Bob and being wiser than I, Bob suggested I call "that younger girl" we had met in the upstate wedding. He urged me into the phone booth of The Brown Derby, one of our favorite haunts in downtown Poughkeepsie.

As I closed the folding door of the now obsolete utility. I thought, "what are the chances?" The sweetie that I had met by chance was now the recipient of a chance call. Should I begin with "Would you by chance be free Saturday night?" The phone rang and after identifying myself to her cautious father, Lisa got on the phone and seemed surprised that I was calling. The wheels were set in motion.

My car, in those days, was a '53 VW bug that had begun to rust out. Its faded blue paint had taken on a corroded look. It had a sunroof that opened with a turn of a handle that revealed a thin rubber seal which, it was hoped would keep out the rain. There was a turn handle emergency gas tank that offered two extra gallons when needed but I, with my graduate student intelligence, kept it open so I would be surprised when I ran out of gas. The heater had cracked pipes under the hood which of course was really the trunk, so I had to stuff a towel in the glove compartment to cut down on drafts. My beloved bug was very far from being a "chick magnet." Fortunately, I had a back up. My college R.A. and close friend had an apartment in Albany, where I not only could crash but borrow his car, a '65 VW which was in good shape. It was only a short drive to Lisa's family home from there.

So here was the second time a good friend had aided me in my latest romantic sojourn. His apartment was a graduate student den of post-undergraduate life. It was furnished in early Salvation Army. One roommate was away for the weekend, so I got his bare mattress on the floor. The kitchen highlights included beer cans and an oven that smoked due to various entrees being baked on the stove racks. Apparently, there were no pans. Ed had a very respectable job with the State. His roommate was a doctoral bio student, La Fountain who was a runner and indeed ran in and out all hours, maybe from research work or activity with a co-ed. He was nicknamed the Fountainhead. Ed shared one of his two towels with me in case I dared to take a shower in the tub that had perhaps been cleaned the year before.

After a quick sandwich with Ed, a re-shave and a change of clothes, I was off to pick up "the younger girl" and meet the family. A short drive over the

Menands Bridge and up the hill past HVCC, I soon found Meadow Drive and licked my dry lips before ringing the doorbell on the well cared for, 1950's ranch house. I was from the inner city of old Poughkeepsie and had not dated a "suburban"girl. The large yards echoed farmland, now developed for the commuters to Troy and Albany. The door opened to a smiling thin man, his short white hair was combed in waves similar to my older brother's. "Hi Rich!" I'm Lisa's dad Tom, but you can call me Mack." Just as quickly, a thin lady with a warm inviting smile appeared, wiping her hands on an apron.

Her Mom, Nancy, had a charm and a smile that didn't go away. Her eyes twinkled . The smell of cigarettes filled the air but the welcome of her parents made me less aware of it. We sat for a few moment in the living room while they questioned me about who I was and did I deserve to be taking out the innocent beauty, their daughter. From the other room came the sounds of a horse race about to begin. Mack, as he was called, was ordered to turn off the OTB show that he had on. As years passed I knew him to have the betting show on all the time, while filling up the ashtray in front of him.

Soon the front door opened and a slight young fellow in a Catholic High jacket entered, a book bag slung over one shoulder. "Larry, this is Rich. He's your sister's date." The very Irish looking kid gave me a perfunctory handshake and slipped away as fast as he could. "Larry's a sophomore and his sister has been unsuccessful at socializing him as of yet, " Nance explained.

I glanced in Lisa's direction and smiled. She cued me by quickly standing and signaling it was time. While trying not to look too eager, I held her jacket and gave the Mc's the usual banter about how great it was to meet them and I hoped to see them again to which Nance responded, "Oh, I bet that won't be a problem." I smiled and walked with Lis to Ed's car to hold the door. As I rounded the VW they stood in the door and waved happily. Another good omen. I hardly spoke to most parents of my dates and often they would quickly rush us out the door. I felt different vibes all the way round.

The rest of the night is a blur now years later but I do know that as we walked, I put my hand lightly on the small of her back and I felt electric.

Ice cream at a Troy coffee shop and the return to Meadow Drive followed. We walked to her front porch and she strategically went up two steps to balance our height difference. She smiled and said, "We might have some potential." I leaned forward to match up with her lips, a result much better than my first attempt. "No doubt," I smiled. "No doubt about it."

Chance had crowned me.

Dream Folly

5A.M.

I wake to chirping of our avian neighbors.

> Our open window lets in the green outdoors, and sunshine invades our bed.

It breaks apart the early morning gray

> That fills the bedroom and my head.

Moments ago, I touched and whispered to assorted girls I dated long ago.

> In young ardor I thought it love but what I dream of is expired heat.

Wrestled kisses and awkward groping looking in vain for their secrets.

> In this early morning flashback, they love me and I them.

But these evanescent scenes vanish in the light of day

> replaced by the sleeping figure lying close to me for many years.

Her curves hidden under sheets and covers; her flowing hair now pillow wrapped.

> A composite of those girls I knew, perhaps, but real love not the starry eyed love of youth

> No folly but rather a dream fulfilled.

Irish Love Song

The sweet taste of rambling together was made sweeter

    by this ancient land of brown bread and honey,'

By smiles and laughs from Antrim to Shannon, from Dun Laoghrie to Claire.

    Just us three, the country you and me.

A tiny Fiat and the narrow road was ours

    Stone walls and peat piled high criss crossed the rolling hills.

When stopped, goats would amble by to stare at us,

    Now and then, the sheep, heavy with wool marked with paint, halted the car.

Under rain filled skies we toured ruined abbeys, looked in silence at church graveyards

    With stones pocked by moldering green.

We gazed in wonder at Norman towers that saved Irish from Viking raids,

    And stood arms around each other imagining fearful farmers running for safety.

The B&B, our refuge from the damp, drew us back like home,

    To the warmth of tea and scones,

To the warmth of the peat fire and a dram of whiskey,

    And each other.

Cape Magic

Stars float over the bay,

    their glow lightens the twinkling shoreline.

How many couples lie together somewhere in the dunes

    Eyes skyward while hands caress the earth?

The North star and Ursa Major seem to wink at each other

    Could there be a liaison in the galaxies?

Head bent back, eyes to the heavens, I'm enchanted

    As though awaiting a kiss.

The salty air as warm as the anticipation of a waiting lover.

    Transformed, the beach and bay disappear under a star-filled blanket.

Rising from my sandy bed as if from a dream,

    I rub the stardust from my eyes and smile after such a consummation with the cosmos.

Sea Spray

The beach stretched before them disappearing in the early morning haze.

> The surf slapped at their feet, erasing footprints as they walked.

Terns and gulls scattered as they approached, skittering off and on the sand

> or flapping into the blue.

Hand in hand or always just in reach, the two stepped in and out of the swirling waters

> As if dancing back and forth with the bay,

In synch with the ancient ebb and flow of the tide.

> She smiled at him as if she had a secret and glanced up and down the shore.

Gracefully she raised one foot then the next, and slipped from her shorts

> Handed them off to him and before he could say a word,

Like a half-naked child she pranced into the deepening water,

> With shining hips and thighs now kissed by the sun,

Squatted quickly and joined her stream with the laughing ocean around her.

Brewster Flats

The world stands still at low tide.

> The skirt of water is lifted until the floor of the Bay is revealed.

Water and sand alternate in long strips of color spread out before the bluffs.

> Many walkers leave the beach to explore the newly opened shallows

To stroll into the horizon, until the waters finally deepen.

> They diminish in size to those left behind on dry land until they become spots on the

edge of the world.

> They may be in Europe before long.

Sounds of people a mile off can be heard as clear as the chirping of birds on shore.

    Life is softened by this new, still world

The ebb has occurred, the flow will follow as it has for a thousand years,

    One of nature's certainties.

Eternal, we hope, constant as day and night, clouds and sunlight.

    Greens of tall grasses blur in a gentle breeze.

Marshy puddles full of broken shells and pebbles.

    Skittering hermit crabs who have escaped the pillaging birds.

All await the rising of the tide.

From Plymouth to P-Town

From Plymouth to P-Town, the Bay is lit with fire.

    Almost blinded at first, the shaded worshippers of sunset

File onto the shore complete with their bottles, wine glasses and snacks

    To share communion in the sand.

Fully ablaze, the solar show commences.

    It begins its drop to the sea, filling the blue with gold.

The edge of the world is lit as the orb plants a kiss on the earth.

    Color runs into color.

The setting sun inches slowly at first.

    And then...and then it is half extinguished in the edge

Between sky and sea.

We blink and it is has faded into the misty horizon.

The last trace of light turns the Cape pink.

    A collective toast to the show is heard resounding down the shore.

To life, now one day shorter.

    Our glasses are emptied and dark has come.

Old cliches abound- How beautiful!, Nothing like the Cape!

    Folded chair in one hand, wine glass in the other

We climb the dune toward the porch lights of clustered cottages.

    The sundown now a night lite.

    Another closing on the Bay.

Without

On October 2, 2015, Lisa succumbed to the lung cancer that she fought so well for almost four years. Trips for treatments and hundreds, or so it seemed, of tests at home or at Dana Farber failed to weaken her resolve. She laughed and loved life through it all until the final days. On the day she died at home, several close friends were gathered to see her and share time. When the wine was poured in the living room, Lisa was in her bed and remarked that she was missing the party. A Sauvignon Blanc was brought to her bedside and we had a toast. Not long after, she slipped away. That was Lisa.

These poems were written during the following year and were inspired partly by the work of Donald Hall whose beautiful collection of poems, Without, was written to his wife, Jane Kenyon.

They helped me get through the process and I hope, convey something of my own experience of grieving.

A Run

I run in place, waking early to a solitary life.

    I seek escape, and so to church.

The place, the mood lends itself to silent sobbing over a grief touching my soul.

    I feel a calm, a temporary comfort in ritual and song

And then I'm off

    To talk to friends and to the communion of coffee.

Once more, I run from this sanctuary

    Into the comfortable din of the diner,

To lose myself in french toast and papers.

    The solitary house awaits my return,

the humming of the furnace, and the creaking of floors and silent spaces.

    I stare at the snow covered woods from my rear window and I know what I must do-

jog into a future; the course still unclear

    Toward finish lines not yet determined.

No trophies, or breaking a tape, no win or lose,

    Just the need to run.

Flannel Dreams

A foggy morning silently welcomes me

    Like a blanket thrown over my mind

Thinking through flannel and wool, my thoughts are warmed

    As sleeping children tucked into bed, secured.

"Life is a dream", it's been said

    And so now are my thoughts of you.

A dream of mourning tiptoes over my pillow:

    Last days, nurses and memorial stones come and go.

A part always of me, but not me.

But still a night vision that will not let me go.

    To wrest free from it I must make dreams as light as cotton,

Block out the dark things and smile at all the happy moments

    That can never be undreamt:

The travels, the celebrations, the children that carry life on.

    These can still keep me warm and sure

And raise me from the fog of loss

    And wake me wrapped in a new, shining morning.

A Gray Day in December

Only two months gone.

    A loss that seems forever.

It's a passing that has dulled my senses,

    Numbed my feelings, and cast my thoughts adrift like a boat broken away from its dock.

My soul is an island not to be reached

    No one can know the hurt, but one who has lost a life so close, a loss that makes the

gray days longer.

    In a world now out of joint, I step over the cracks,

    jump over the gaps, less I am lost,

Swallowed up in the gray light of year's end.

Frozen Redeemer

The cemetery where you lie is hushed under the blanket of cold rain.

    A city of stones rises on the flat green land.

Memorials as they are called by the purveyors of plots and solace.

    All is under the watch of the three storied columbarium on the edge of the woods.

Grass sprouts, the only thing to grow in the now cold season, mark your grave which awaits

    the stone and our shared epitaph.

My thoughts are soft whispers and my eyes dampen like the day.

    "Love's not time's fool" rises up to join the misty air.

Westport: The First Thanksgiving

The first Thanksgiving

The cold blue Long Island Sound fills the window

    And sunset makes rosey the end of day.

An empty chair at the first holiday.

    Survivors gather round the festive table to raise a glass

To life that is and was and you.

    Our world, regardless, inches on.

Grief subsides to a calm like the bay outside.

    A sip of wine helps numb our loss and makes the sun seem more warm.

We're bound by love and a faith unspoken.

    Here in a new place, a new feeling,

A new found strength, we never sought or wanted.

Chant

Snow now covers the graveyard in a thin January blanket.

    Stones are framed in white, frozen memories of life.

Christmas wreaths still dot the landscape; they stand out on what was in the fall, still green.

    Summer is long gone.

The warmth was lost to passing time, as were you.

    An icy breeze wafts from the west and we shiver.

We pull on our hoods, a futile try to extend our wintry visit to the plot.

    The occasional car that passes, might think us monks,

Huddling over a grave of the departed,

    The deceased, a body once of this earth, now gone.

I imagine a chanted prayer for you,

    for us,

        for all who feel your loss.

And shudder with the cold, and mortal thoughts.

Winter Limbo (January 2015)

    I chill. I stiffen, I flex in vain to keep my aging body loose.

My mind, almost as cold, my thoughts rise slowly in the winter air

    past the woodscape of stark leafless trees.

I hibernate in the warm cave of my house and slip away in flights of fancy:

    to sunny beaches

        to an ocean, blue and breaking

            to better days.

My thoughts fly with the updrafts of sun filled air:

    away from the frozen ground

        away from the graveyards of January

            away from mortality.

And I am redeemed by what the world still offers:

    A smile, a sensuous chardonnay and friendship.

Layers

I blanket my feelings with activity

    And run through events that people say must be fun.

At first.

    I remain stoic when receiving sympathy from the wives of friends,

Consolatory hugs from strangers.

    I layer myself by being a "hale brother well met,"

To stifle the silence of a still hearth and home.

    I pause to rest my feet, and for a moment, think--

Then rush into the world of wine and song where women smile and pass,

    And leave me numb.

Like a Russian doll, who hides other dolls within,

    My smaller and smaller lives stay secret to all but me.

Naples FL: A Winter Reverie

A beautiful solitude at times.

    Greens of the earth, the tan of the sand,

The sun filled ocean and sky are one.

    All warm my body, still cold from northern nights.

Yet I wait for it to warm my soul.

Quiet days are on me like a blanket thrown over my face.

    I may be warm, but can't breathe

A chat with a bartender or listening to the chatter of my retired neighbors

    With whom I can share wine, but not my feelings is my society.

I call a grieving cousin who is planning a year of memories and joy

    In celebration of her husband's life.

A worthy cause but not yet for me.

    I long for home, a cold empty house

Still new to us, even newer to me, alone.

    You passed through on your way.

So I who lived for us, must now live for ours

    And whatever I can be; to marvel at the earth, the sea, the sky

And see you there.

Emotional Rescue

I need to be an exile,

> to lose myself in sun filled beaches and ocean sounds, to be marooned on the sand.

I cast myself from cold weather and colder feelings,

> From a passing most profound,

that rises and falls within me as the waves on the shore.

> The beauty which surrounds me touches my broken soul, but fails to heal.

Nature laughs at our human frailty and continues on and on with or without us.

> Being alone makes cold a summer day;

without you, or friends or roots, I drift, I slip into numbness.

> I hold back a call for help, a call to save myself and instead-

I recall the love that was, that still is and the one which still could be.

> To carry this love on the rest of the journey, strengthens my resolve ,

To endure, even to the edge, without need for rescue.

> "If this be error and upon me proved,
> I never writ nor no man ever loved."
>
> Sonnet XVI

A Smile Once More

Thanks to the Bard

When I remember all that I could see,
    Through eyes made brighter by a woman's smile,
That caused my pulse to stop and then to race
    With thoughts of love that quickly turned toward lust
Without you here, such moods have turned to dust.
How to return to senses now asleep?
    Your sound, your scent, your smile, your special state
Return to me in dreams that will endure
    And when a passing woman smiles on me and warms my aging frame,
My fantasies explode
    My mind's eye sees you smile and once again my feelings soar.

Thoughts From the Pew

Early for Mass I sit in the near-empty church

    A children's choir rehearsing.

So many feelings here you'd have liked-

    Innocent voices, little bell swingers and drum thumpers.

To sit here surrounded by light of the stained glass.

    Outside the cold of early April,

The sanctuary fills with the joy of music, warming the chilly void.

Some miles away silk flowers on the gravesite between our names, an attempt to bring rebirth

    To the stark cemetery.

A splash of color, a splash of joy

    Like the singing of children filling an empty church.

The stained glass on the stairs of my childhood home

> Shone as we entered the house like a churchly star above us.

A miniature church window bringing light to a dark hall.

> Church windows behind me and before me lighten my darkest thoughts-

Of life and death, of living and dying with a dream of immortality

> Colors wash the empty pews in pious blue, holy green and joyous red.

Spirits rise in cathedral awe.

Seeking

Seeking you in Starbucks,

    I check all those who enter,

But see only unfamiliar faces.

    Armed with but a hot cup.

I look and look again.

    No feeling here but loneliness in a crowd of people;
    I'm lost in space.

Lost as well at night in darkness,

    My only mates are ghostly shadows cast by
    the nitelight.

I seek you out in dreams of where we were or where

    we might have been and wake to silence.

My morning coffee allows me to see more clearly the gap that is my life.

    Alone,

I'm free to move, if I dare

    To imagine a place where searching ceases.

When the silence of time can be refilled with wonder

    of what still might be and

What is to come can be almost as good as what was.

Cuba Libre

An island very close, yet locked in time by guns
and missiles.

> People haven't posed a risk, only leaders caught up
> by power.

Never wanting to blink first, a wall was built, unlike
Frost's wall,

> It kept something in.

The beauty of family and music; a wonder at the sea, the
birds, the land, their island.

> A love of baseball and 1950's cars- the beauty of a
> 52 convertible

> Speeding along the Maracon, sea spray breaking
> high above.

An adventure like no other.

> My fellow travelers buzz with the rush of learning.

To ramble with pals is good, but with a lover better.

> Cuba would have shown its magic, its mystery.

She and I found in Ireland, Italy, France

> In England and Spain we shared a shoulder, hands, a kiss.

Now all pleasant memories.

And yet, she travels with me through the challenge of rocky streets, parching heat

> And aches and pains of an aging road warrior.

"Oh look." I say out loud. In the flores bonita, I see her.

> In the history we touch, I hear her.

In the sounds of Cuban music, I feel her.

She looks with sympathy at the gnawing streets of poverty,

At the leathered face of life in wind swept fishing villages.

> And the shoeless children kicking around what once was a soccer ball.

I wish I could share my thoughts and wonder.

> But I can only daydream, of her eyes over Cuba.

Sunsets for Christmas

I mark the years by sunrises of Christmas past.

> Days of expectation and celebration, gifts from God that quickly passed.

And even when memories scatter like needles under the tree, they reappear in

> The corners of my thoughts:

The sunrise over a pile of presents and new bike, in 1953.

> Shone on a Schwinn big tire, horn beeping beauty.

It leaned jauntily against my grandmother's living room wall.

> The Christmas mornings I rushed downstairs to see the cookies left for Santa reduced to crumbs,

The tree surrounded by boxes wrapped in the Sunday comics or brown paper bags.

> A December 25th, that began with a drunken decoration of the tree the eve before,

My older brother having cut the top off the tree, too tall to fit the room.

> Decorating with a girlfriend, whose kisses warmed the colors of lights and ornaments.

> That bright Christmas morning when a diamond waited in my pocket to put sunlight in her eyes.

The fondue and love to celebrate a time we never dreamed would set

> Kids sneaking down the stairs to find gifts that came with the morning light

Before we knew it, back from college they came to share yet again, with one foot out the door.

> Now alone, I visit our children's children to watch the cycle continue

And when the celebration wanes, the opened gifts lie strewn round the tree

> The still glowing coals in the fireplace burn down

As red as the setting sun, still aflame through the snow laden pines.

The Close

Last days are most painful,

    Lives severed by divorce, by change of heart or by life and death

Conclude as a puzzle that has lost pieces,

    a picture that can never be restored.

A broken chalice that will never hold water or wine.

    A body that is getting close to not holding life.

The once beloved doctor slipped into the hospital room, like a burglar about to take your

    valuables.

"There's nothing more we can do" and without even a goodbye hug escaped our life.

    No "Bon Voyage" for him, no "Have a good one."

We're alone in our own confusion;

    you to pain-killers, me to tears and helplessness.

Chapter by Chapter

Metaphors for life abound.

    A journey, an odyssey, a quest

"Two roads" or a "poor player that struts and frets his hour upon the stage."

    Perhaps my life as a reader has led me to see life as a novel.

Consider me a hardcover tale that blends many strands in Dickensian style.

    A somber introduction, but a happy plot development.

Elements of rainbows and smiles, of heartbreak and tears intersect.

    The setting is the heart and the time eternal.

The action is both comic and tragic, with both love and loss.

    There's a protagonist that must adjust or be defeated.

And if the storyline seems to ramble, it is redirected, and focused

    By the magic of friends or perhaps a renewed love.

And redeemed by the love of children and grandchildren,

> Or the grandeur of the mountains and the beauty of the blue green sea.

The resolution of the conflict comes like the sunrise,

> Harkening the end of darkness and the return of light

My novel is like a tale the reader can't put down, but must.

> And when the book is closed the bittersweet feeling of hours well spent,

Prevails.

Acknowledgements

Thanks to my daughter, Sara, for helping me find my balance when I most needed it. Thanks to my son, Chris, for being my pal. Thanks to Marie, a new-old love.

Thanks to Dr. Paul O'Brien

Sonnet 73 by William Shakespeare

That time of year thou may'st in me behold
When yellow leaves or none, or few do hang
Upon those boughs which shake against the cold,
Bare ruined choirs, where late the sweet birds sang.
In me thou see'st the twilight of such day
As after sunset fadeth in the west;
Which by and by black night doth take away
Death's second self, that seals up all in rest.

In me thou see'st the glowing of such fire,
That on the ashes of his life doth lie,
As on the deathbed whereon it must expire,
Consumed with that which it was nourished by.
This thou perceive'st, which makes thy love more strong,
To love that well which thou must leave ere long.